Contents

Managing Editor: Rex Kennedy
Editorial Team:
Andrew Kennedy and Andrew Wilson
Design: Ian Kennedy

Editorial
PO Box 2471, Bournemouth BH7 7WF
Telephone/Fax: 01202 304849
e-mail: red.gauntlett@btconnect.com

Publishing
Managing Director: Adrian Cox
Executive Chairman: Richard Cox
Commercial Director: Ann Saundry
Group Marketing Manager: Martin Steele
Webmaster: Simon Russell

Published by: Key Publishing Ltd,
PO Box 100, Stamford, Lincs. PE9 1XP
Repro: pkmediaworks@mac.com
Print: Precision Colour Printing Ltd,
Haldane, Halesfield 1, Telford, Shropshire
TF7 4QQ
Distribution: Seymour Distribution Ltd,
2 Poultry Avenue, London EC1A 9PP

Cover: **'West Country Pacific No 34096
Trevone climbs to Honiton tunnel east with
a westbound express in May 1959.**
K. Pir*t*/Courtesy Book Law Publications

This page: **No 35008 *Orient Line* on a down
express overhauls BR '5MT' 4-6-0 No 73082
Camelot on a down local train near
Farnborough in September 1963.**
K. Pir*t*/Courtesy Book Law Publications

5 INTRODUCTION

6 FROM STEAM TO ELECTRIFICATION:

   THE PLANNED DECLINE OF STEAM ON THE SOUTHERN

14 SPECIAL TRAFFIC ON THE SOUTHERN

30 FAWLEY OIL TRAFFIC

38 MODIFYING THE BULLEID PACIFICS

47 CLAPHAM JUNCTION IN THE 1960s

56 SOUTHAMPTON BOAT TRAINS

65 THE GIESL 'SPAM-CANS'

71 STEAM DAYS IN COLOUR:

   THE SOUTHERN'S 'WITHERED ARM'

77 THE SOUTHERN REGION'S LAST STEAM SHEDS

89 THE SOUTHERN REGION'S BR STANDARDS

97 THE LYMINGTON BRANCH

   BR'S LAST STEAM-OPERATED BRANCH LINE

104 SOUTHERN REGION RAILTOURS

108 THE PENULTIMATE WEEKEND OF SOUTHERN STEAM

'Merchant Navy' class Pacific No 35001 *Channel Packet* at Stewarts Lane shed, Battersea, carrying the 'Night Ferry' headboard on 8 September 1957. The 'Night Ferry' was the through service from London (Victoria) to Paris (Nord) via the Dover-Dunkerque train ferry. With its *Wagon-Lits* sleeping cars, the 'Night Ferry' was the heaviest passenger train on British Railways. R. C. Riley

Introduction

Scheduled steam services on British Railways (Southern Region) ended fifty years ago on 9 July 1967, although on the Isle of Wight steam-hauled services had ended on 31 December 1966. It was always the aim of the Southern and its constituent companies to electrify as many of their lines as possible from the start, when the London, Brighton & South Coast Railway opened its first electric service over the South London line in 1909. This was followed by the London & South Western Railway's electrification of some of its suburban lines in 1915. The LB&SCR operated the 6,600volt ac overhead system and the L&SWR used 650volt third rail. So the writing was always on the wall for the elimination of steam on its lines as electrification on the region continued with the Kent Coast electrification schemes in the 1960s and the electrification of the L&SWR main line to Bournemouth and Weymouth in the later 1960s.

The electrification schemes resulted in the cascading down of steam locomotives to non-electrified routes, and at the 1923 Grouping the Southern Railway was formed from the amalgamation of the London, Chatham & Dover Railway, the London, Brighton & South Coast Railway, the London South Western Railway, the South Eastern Railway, the Southern Eastern & Chatham Railway, the narrow-gauge Lynton & Barnstaple Railway, the Freshwater, Yarmouth & Newport Railway on the Isle of Wight, and the Plymouth, Devonport & South Western Junction Railway, and many locomotives from these pre-Grouping companies survived into BR (Southern Region) days when the railways were nationalized on 1 January 1948.

Like other regions of British Railways the Southern Region had a variety of freight workings, passenger services and special traffic over the years, such as Derby Day race-goer trains, the hop-pickers' trains, and those of the hop-pickers' friends who travelled in special trains to visit friends and families at weekends in the hop fields, a unique service, not just for the Southern Region, but also the Western Region to the hop-fields in Herefordshire. Other 'Special Traffic' included the milk trains to pasteurising and bottling plants at Vauxhall and Morden South in London from the West Country each day, and the perishables traffic from the Channel Isles and bananas from Jamaica arriving at Weymouth and Southampton. Then there was the car-carrier train from Surbiton to Okehampton in Devon in the early 1960s that, much to the delight of its users, avoided the huge traffic jams on the Honiton and Exeter by-passes.

Another interesting form of traffic was the boat trains to and from Southampton Docks and those through Kent to Dover such as the 'Night Ferry' and the 'Golden Arrow', and in this survey of Southern steam we take a look at the Southampton boat trains from Waterloo, prolific in the mid-1950s, that met ships arriving from and departing to destinations far and wide, such as South Africa and South America, in addition to cross-channel and Channel Isles services.

Oil from Fawley in Hampshire, was a very important commodity that was transported over Southern metals from the Hampshire refinery to Birmingham and the north, some of it over the old Didcot, Newbury & Southampton Railway route, and the four Kent coalfields were busy with coal trains heading to and from London and the Kent coast. A variety of motive power could be seen on all these trains, especially those working over the Fawley branch and the East Kent Railway.

We show what it was like for the railway enthusiast spending a day in and around Clapham Junction in the 1960s in an interesting nostalgic photo-feature from those days, and also provide an all-colour photo-feature showing the variety of motive power and trains that could be witnessed from the lineside on the Southern Region's lines in the West Country.

We then take a look at some of the modifications that were made to locomotives constructed by Southern Railway at their locomotive Works at Eastleigh, Brighton and Ashford, these including those made to Bulleid's Pacific locomotives following the derailment of the 'Merchant Navy' Pacific at Crewkerne in 1953, when streamlined casings were removed, and the fitting of the Geisl ejector system to Southern Light Pacific No 34064 *Fighter Command,* which is fully explained here.

The Southern Region also used a good cross section of BR Riddles designs from 'Britannia' Pacifics to the '2MT' 2-6-2Ts, and as the end of steam on the region approached, many rail tours were run, using a variety of Southern steam locomotives. Sadly as more and more Southern steam engines were withdrawn we saw the sorry sight of lines and lines of Southern engines in the scrapyards of South Wales, but all was not lost as from those long lines of engines rotting away on those scraplines around thirty Southern Pacific locomotives were saved from the cutter's torch to start new lives at preserved railway sites in Britain, in addition to locomotives from other classes, some from pre-Grouping railway companies, so Southern steam lives on for us all to still enjoy today.

Adams 'O2' class 0-4-4T No W22 *Brading* **approaches Ryde (St. John's Road) station with a train for Ventnor on 13 September 1964.** Roy Hobbs

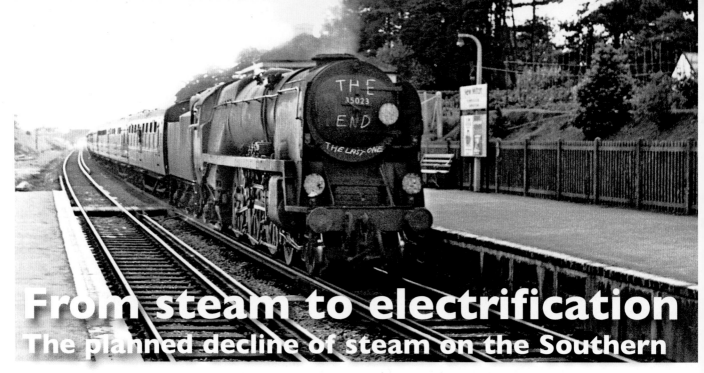

From steam to electrification
The planned decline of steam on the Southern

Jeremy English *relates the progress of the Southern Railway and Southern Region of British Railways in the electrification of as many lines as possible in the south of England.*

On Saturday, 8 July 1967, 'Merchant Navy' class Pacific No 35023 – still *Holland-Afrika Line* to the enthusiasts – is pictured pounding through New Milton station in Hampshire with the last steam-hauled up 'Channel Island Boat Express' (the 15.55 Weymouth to Waterloo service), the sad chalked markings recording 'The End'. However, little did the sad observers of this train know that it wasn't 'The Last One' as the smaller inscription said, because its sister locomotive, No 35030 *Elder Dempster Lines,* which had taken the actual last down train out of Waterloo a few hours earlier, would substitute for a failed diesel the very next day and return triumphantly to Waterloo once again. Nigel Kendall/Platform 14 NK0246

The words 'The End – The Last One' proclaimed the chalked-on message on the smokebox door of rebuilt Bulleid 'Merchant Navy' class No 35023 as it pulled up to the buffers in the early evening at Waterloo on 8 July 1967. Heading both down and up Channel Islands boat trains that day the message was clear – there would be no more Southern steam thereafter — but there was! On Sunday, 9 July a diesel at Weymouth failed before the 14.07 Weymouth to Waterloo express departed, and the last 'Merchant Navy' class Pacific, No 35030, (all names had been removed) just happened to still be in steam and took over the train, running right through to Waterloo, receiving chalk marks stating it was the 'Last Steam'. That was it — the end of the end.

If the end seemed to have been a drawn out, when had it started? When was the beginning of the end? Surprisingly, it was 1 December 1909, and it had taken nearly 60 years to complete. On that day the London, Brighton & South Coast Railway (LB&SCR) inaugurated its first electric service over the South London line, and the first steam locomotives on any of the four great railways which would comprise the Southern Railway and British Railways (Southern Region) became redundant.

Of course, the actual locomotives displaced by the South London electrification didn't get scrapped – they replaced much older ones elsewhere which did get scrapped, a process later to be termed 'cascading'. But after that day the LB&SCR didn't build another steam locomotive for suburban passenger work and, in the remaining thirteen years of its existence, it only built another 35 passenger steam locomotives, all for express work.

The second major event in the elimination of Southern steam came on 25 October 1915 when the London & South Western Railway (L&SWR) inaugurated its electrification of suburban lines. Again, no more suburban locomotives were built thereafter, the last one being a Drummond 'M7' class 0-4-4T, No 481, in December 1911.

The Managing Committee of the South Eastern (SER) and London, Chatham & Dover (SE&CR) railways was too poor to fund any electrification, but it did supply the Southern Railway at its formation in 1923 with a very significant senior employee, one Alfred Raworth, who became the senior electrification manager. It also provided the Southern with its first Chief Mechanical Engineer, Richard Maunsell, whose steam locomotive production for the Southern was very circumscribed by the over-riding policy of its General Manager,

The LB&SCR, or 'Brighton', electrics were some of the most advanced trains of their time. Although they were to be superseded by the L&SWR third-rail electrics when the Southern took over in 1923, and made the latter its standard for the massive Southern electric network, the 'Brighton' pioneered overhead 25hz single-phase ac operation which foreshadowed the later BR standard form of electrification, common today, This wasn't quite such a far-sighted policy as it may seem – 25hz single-phase ac was simply the power output of the local power stations on the South London line! The trains themselves were also pioneering, being multiple-units with as much of the superstructure devoted to passenger accommodation as possible, and no separate locomotives. The last units produced, under the Southern, would have separate motor cars, but 'Brighton' ones did not.

The 'Brighton' had built many varieties of tank engines for suburban services, but no more were constructed after the inauguration of electrification. The 'E4' class Radial 0-6-2Ts were effectively mixed traffic machines so they were simply re-assigned to goods traffic as seen here at Purley where No 559 heads a down goods train under the wires.

The L&SWR's third-rail system was considerably easier and cheaper to install, so when Herbert Walker, a former L&SWR man, became General Manager of the Southern with the ambition to electrify almost everything, he standardised on the system he knew best. Obviously, for some time, steam and electric had to run alongside one another and this view of an Adams '415' class 4-4-2T on 6-wheel suburban stock kept for workmen's trains clearly shows the third rail in place, whilst the old tank engine (also known as a Radial tank) rattles along through Clapham Cutting at Earlsfield with the chimneys of the Durnsford Road power station at Wimbledon in the background. The power station here was specifically built by the L&SWR for its electrification, so it was thus able to choose its own supply standards, this being 600volt dc system.

Herbert Walker. If Walker had had his own way, Southern steam would have been over before the middle of the 20th century, but circumstances, notably the shenanigans and ambitions of a certain Austrian former army corporal, curtailed Walker's own ambitions.

The LB&SCR suburban electrification operated a 6,600V ac overhead system, but the L&SWR system was 650V dc third rail. The Southern Railway, on its formation in 1923, eyed up the options and eventually decided to go with third rail, so a period of consolidation ensued while the Brighton electrified lines were converted to third rail. Some routes changed over on 17 June 1928, with the remaining section going on 22 September 1929.

The LB&SCR had planned to extend electrification to its own main line to Brighton

Steam and electric trains were often seen together, but this view at Brighton station in 1933 was photographed to show just how far propulsion on the Southern Railway had come upon the inauguration of the first main-line electrification. A new Maunsell electric unit was paraded alongside the famous William Stroudley 0-4-2 express locomotive *Gladstone* that was now redundant and about to be preserved by the Stephenson Locomotive Society. O.J. Morris/Lens of Sutton Collection

The Continental boat trains had always been prestige services but somewhat awkward to schedule due to vagaries of the tides and shipping in general. Both Maunsell and Bulleid were tasked with designing powerful steam locomotive types with these trains in mind, and Maunsell's version was the 'Lord Nelson' class which briefly became the most powerful express steam locomotives on Britain's railways, in theory at least. Sadly they seldom lived up to expectations and were subjected to many design modifications. Only sixteen were built, and here we see No 863 *Lord Rodney* at Hildenborough on an up 'Continental' boat train in 1939 sporting Bulleid's multiple blastpipe chimney which was his main contribution to making useful engines out of them.

Maunsell's only new express steam locomotives in the 1930s were the forty engines of what was probably his best design of all, the 'V' or 'Schools' class of 4-4-0s. Like Drummond before him, his 4-cylindered engines were not a spectacular success, but his reversion to a 4-coupled layout created exactly the opposite, as these engines are regarded as probably the finest 4-4-0s of all on Britain's railways. No 918 *Hurstpierpoint* is appropriately seen on a Hastings line train at Chelsfield on an unknown date as loading gauge restrictions on that line had a major influence on the design of the 'Schools' class 4-4-0s. Most noticeable was the use of a round-top firebox derived from the 'N15 King Arthur' design, rather than the very long Belpaire type used on the 'Lord Nelsons' which were the latter's 'Achilles Heel'.

Maunsell's principal express steam locomotives were his 'King Arthur' class 4-6-0s, No E765 *Sir Gareth* pictured here on an up 'Continental' boat train at Dover (Marine) in 1926. The 'E' in its number is significant, as it indicates that this was an Eastleigh-designed and maintained class. These locomotives were not really a new Southern design but were an update of the 20-strong 'N15' class produced by Robert Urie for the L&SWR after World War I, although Maunsell made some major modifications to the valve gear to make the 'King Arthurs' considerably better than the 'N15' class engines; the Southern built just 54 of them.

and once third rail was standardised this eventually took place in 1933, becoming the third major nail in the coffin for Southern steam. Walker's plan was to electrify all of the Southern's main lines, and by 1939 most of the important Brighton lines were sparked, and the former L&SWR Portsmouth main line had electric trains. The first part of electrification in Kent had taken place, and the main lines to Dover via Tonbridge and Chatham were next on the list. It all came to a grinding halt on 3 September 1939.

One aspect of Southern train working which distinguished it from the other three great railways was that passenger traffic was paramount, and freight was a very poor relation. Due to the high concentration of passenger traffic during the daytime most freight was run at night. This affected the kind of steam locomotives that were required by the company; most had to work passenger trains in the daytime and freight trains at night, so there was a preponderance of mixed traffic locomotives. During Maunsell's tenure only sixteen 'Lord Nelson' and 64 'King Arthur' class 4-6-0s and forty 'Schools' class

Bulleid's controversial Pacific locomotives sidled into service during the darkest days of World War II, designated as mixed traffic machines, although they were most usually used of heavy passenger expresses. Much of their development took place under the cloud of war, and after the war the Southern was to build vast numbers of them, 140 in all, nearly twice as many as had been built to Maunsell's designs for such duties. The seventh Bulleid Pacific to be built, 'Merchant Navy' Pacific No 21C7 *Aberdeen Commonwealth* is seen on the post-war 'Devon Belle' service at Broad Clyst on 26 June 1948, a somewhat bizarre train that took Pullman cars to places on the 'Withered Arm' at weekends. It was really just a way of providing additional stock following war shortages, and only lasted until 1955. The Bulleid Pacifics did actually work quite a number of freight duties but, since these mostly ran at night, they were seldom recorded photographically. Millbrook House Ltd

4-4-0s were built for express passenger work, and even these were often used on van trains at night. A proposed 25-year lifespan would see these locomotives only into the 1950s, by which time electric trains were expected to have taken over. A proposed design for a Bo-Bo electric locomotive was drawn up under Maunsell's regime in 1936.

In the 1930s Raworth planned the mass introduction of electric locomotives for freight work, but also for use on special passenger trains such as boat trains during the day. The peculiarities of the tunnels on the Tonbridge to Hastings line had led the Southern to delay the electrification of that line in 1937, and there is evidence that Raworth intended to use electric locomotives on it, using the existing narrow-profile stock of the steam passenger trains which would then lead on to the elimination of steam.

World War II messed all these plans up. Steam would have to carry on as the principal motive power for some time. Into this cauldron had stepped the second Southern Chief Mechanical Engineer, Oliver Bulleid. Steeped in the steam tradition like his former boss, Nigel Gresley on the LNER, Bulleid was able to seize the opportunity of wartime needs to introduce his own somewhat eccentric idea of a modern steam locomotive which became

the famous 'Merchant Navy' class. Like most Southern steam designs it was described as a mixed traffic locomotive and, indeed, during the war these engines did work heavy goods trains at times. However, Bulleid's first design was an electric locomotive. In conjunction with Raworth, he created the first main line Southern electric locomotive class, a Co-Co design, conceived in 1937 but delayed for technical reasons until 1941. Two were built

Raworth's plans to have hundreds of electric locomotives working on the Southern by the middle of the 20th century were derailed by European hostilities, but he, together with Bulleid, did manage to build three prototypes. A smaller Maunsell version of these, with 4-wheel rather than 6-wheel bogies, had been proposed in 1936, but it was not until the war had started that these three prototypes, with Bulleid's input, appeared. Normally two of the three locomotives worked goods services on the Central Section, with one kept for the Newhaven boat trains, ironically, of course, serving Europe! Here the third member of the trio, BR No 20003 (Bulleid had numbered them CC1 to CC3 in European style) is pictured working one of the latter at Wandsworth Road in 1952.

Again, it was Raworth who predicted diesels for all non-electric work on the Southern, post-war, but it was left to Bulleid to flesh out the design with the considerable help of English Electric who built, again, three prototypes. Appearing after nationalisation these locomotives never had strange Bulleid numbers (would they have been 11CC to 11CC3?) but were always numbered 10201 to 10203 throughout their lives. Although their lives were short – barely ten years – they were really the prototypes of the BR 'Type 4' diesels that had the same wheel arrangement of 1Co-Co1, and were turned out in vast quantities in the late 1950s and 1960s. Ironically, none of the 'Type 4' diesels were ever allocated to the Southern Region. In this scene prototypes Nos 10201 and 10203 are seen near the end of their lives, at Derby in 1962 on the London Midland Region, to which they were transferred in 1955.

(and a third in 1948) and would probably have been the nemesis of steam on the Southern had not the war happened, and had it not led to capital starvation for the railways and eventual nationalisation.

As soon as the war ended, the Southern put out its plans for further electrification, which it anticipated completing by 1955, even though nationalisation was looming. This was based on an internal plan for the future drawn up by Raworth in May 1944, which included a proposal for the building of up to 413 main-line electric locomotives. Due to developments in diesel traction in the U.S.A., diesel locomotives became an option for longer-distance workings (to the West Country in particular). On 31 October 1946 the Southern Board announced 'large-scale plans for the adoption of diesel-electric traction for use in connection with subsidiary lines', and Bulleid was authorised to order three prototypes. It seemed steam was once again on the back burner but Bulleid had somehow also got permission to build 110 of

his 'Lightweight' Pacifics and five prototypes of an extraordinary design known as the 'Leader' class.

In an address to the Institute of Mechanical Engineers on 12 June 1947, Bulleid announced that no less than three new designs of diesel locomotive would figure in future construction, and that the Southern was exploring the possibilities of a gas-turbine locomotive burning coal 'as our natural fuel'. In addition to the Co-Co electrics, a further design for a high-speed electric locomotive was also under consideration. He also gave a few details about the 'Leader'.

The 'Leader' was designed to replace the myriad designs of older steam passenger locomotives such as the SE&CR 'H' and the L&SWR 'M7' classes of 0-4-4Ts, most of which were already forty years or so old. By this time most Brighton steam engines had gone for scrap, and many other pre-Grouping classes were rapidly following them. The failure of the 'Leader' in 1950 led to a crisis in Southern power, especially as the grandiose

plans to continue electrification and dieselisation had been suspended by British Railways. Various former LMS designs and examples of the new BR Standard classes were built for the Southern, but even these weren't sufficient to cope with the crisis, so some obsolescent Southern designs such as the L&SWR Adams Radial tanks and Beattie well tanks had to remain on the books.

Electrification resumed in 1959 when the first phase of electrification in Kent was inaugurated, this being completed in 1962. With BR's version of the Raworth electric locomotives taking on the freight role, this saw a massive cull of steam, with whole classes such as the Brighton 'K' class Moguls, the various SE&CR 4-4-0s, the 'King Arthurs', 'Schools', and 'Lord Nelsons' failing to see out the year.

The final nail in the coffin of steam came as a product of BR's desperate financial state, which resulted in the infamous Beeching Report. Many branch lines and even some important lines such as all of those beyond Salisbury were either slated for total closure or transfer to the Western Region, and this made many more Southern steam locomotives

Had Bulleid had his own way, we might have seen vast quantities of these strange machines across the Southern after the war. He was really a steam man and was constantly trying to improve the classic Stephenson formula. Looking like a cross between a diesel and something from outer space, this is the second 'Leader' dumped unceremoniously at New Cross Gate shed for scrapping before it had even turned a wheel under power. It was just days from completion when the impoverished British Railways decided that Bulleid's experiments were just too extravagant, and terminated the project after a long series of trials with the prototype. These engines were to have replaced Drummond 'M7' and Wainwright 'H' class 0-4-4Ts on secondary services. Brian Morrison

One of the Wainwright engines which had a much longer life than expected ('H' class 0-4-4T No 31520) thanks to the 'Leader' failure, is seen in June 1954 on an up East Grinstead train near Riddlesdown Tunnel South signal box. Quite why Bulleid had thought that these little engines should be replaced by such monstrosities is the stuff of legend and speculation but it left the new Southern Region of British Railways with something of a motive power crisis as the second half of the century unfolded. No doubt the old SE&CR Birdcage stock would have also had to carry on in use, and would have looked quite odd behind a 'Leader'!

redundant. The announcement of electrification to Bournemouth in 1964 was the last straw, and by the beginning of 1967 only some Bulleid Pacifics, some LMS tank engines, and various BR Standard types remained. At 12.00 midnight on that fateful Sunday, 9 July 1967 it was all over.

The solution to the 'Leader'-lead motive power crisis came in the form of a number of '4MT' 2-6-4Ts built at Brighton to a former LMS design by Charles Fairburn, and 41 such machines were built in the Southern's Works there during 1950/51, and were allocated to the semi-cross-country routes based upon Tunbridge Wells West, notably lines through East Grinstead, at whose high-level station where we see No 42103 on 16 March 1957. Two years later the then-remaining examples of the class on the Southern were exchanged for a like number of the BR Standard development of the class. F. Hornby

Here we see one of the BR-built all-electric locomotives built for the Kent Coast Electrification Schemes, primarily for freight work. Classified Type HA (and later TOPS Class 71) the 24 engines of this class were built at Doncaster during 1959/60. They were really an updated version of the Bulleid/Raworth Southern 1930s prototypes and were somewhat late to the show. Originally thirteen of these engines were ordered but, in the revised and accelerated Modernisation Plan panic of 1957, a further eleven were ordered. Sadly, things were changing so rapidly on the railways in the late 1950s that by the time they arrived they were already virtually redundant. The extra eleven locomotives of the class were never needed and ten were converted (very badly) to Class 74 electro-diesels for the Bournemouth Electrification Scheme, which was to spell the end of Southern steam in 1967.

Almost a side-show in the story of the end of Southern Steam is the fate of the lines beyond Salisbury and Exeter, notably the 'Withered Arm' lines. These lines were all handed over to the Western Region at the beginning of 1963, so it was left to that region to either dieselise them or, in most cases, downgrade them, or close them altogether. This left many outposts of the former Southern Railway without any railways from the mid-1960s, even before steam was retired from what was left of the Southern. Here we see what appears to be a perfect Southern scene at Okehampton in Devon, with Maunsell 'N' class Mogul No 31855 prominent. However, the date is 13 July 1963 and the engine, train, and station are no longer Southern, but Western assets. The end of Southern hegemony in the west had come on 1 January of that year. R. Patterson/Colour-Rail 314556

Special traffic on the Southern

Rex Kennedy *takes brief look at four types of special traffic that could be witnessed on the Southern Region in BR days.*

On 16 July 1956 a banana train from Southampton Docks to Nine Elms passes through Eastleigh to begin the climb up through Winchester, the long train being hauled by 'S15' class 4-6-0 No 30838, one of many engines of the class allocated to Feltham shed around this time. Les Elsey

Like all the other regions of British Railways, the Southern Region and, prior to that, the Southern Railway, had its 'special traffic', some of this unfamiliar to most other regions such as the car-carrier trains from the London suburbs to Devon, and the hop-pickers trains in Kent, and trains for their visiting friends and relatives. There were also the milk trains from the West Country to London over Southern metals, and trains conveying fruit, vegetables, and flowers from Weymouth and Southampton that had arrived by boat from the Channel Isles and, at Southampton, from other far-off continents around the world. This pictorial tribute looking at four examples of the Southern's 'special traffic' paints an interesting picture.

Perishables traffic

In pre-Grouping, Southern Railway, and British Railways (Southern Region) days fruit and vegetables arrived from the Channel Isles and other countries in the world, such as South Africa and Jamaica, at the south coast ports of Southampton and Weymouth. However, the port of Weymouth was under the jurisdiction of the GWR until January 1950 when it was transferred over to the Southern Region, although Weymouth's motive power depot remained a Western Region shed until 1958.

The Channel Isles enjoyed a more favourable climate than that on mainland Britain, and we imported the delicious Jersey Royal potatoes and succulent Guernsey tomatoes, favoured products by many families in Great Britain, from there for many years, and these were transported by rail to London and other parts of the United Kingdom. The warm climate in the Channel Isles resulted in potatoes and tomatoes arriving in England quite early, in fact as early as March for those grown under glass. However the main tomato crop arrived from July until early November. French potatoes and broccoli arrived at both Southampton and Weymouth.

In 1956 the Southern Region submitted a proposal to purchase four new ships for the perishables traffic, but it was late in 1958 when it was decided that the Southampton perishables traffic was unprofitable, so the entire Channel Isles perishables traffic was then concentrated on Weymouth. Mechanised loading from ship to train took place in the early 1960s, and more improvements were made from 1962 with better

forms of packaging to help speed up the loading of produce on to ventilated and fruit vans on the trains. Around this time tomatoes left Weymouth for Yorkshire, the north-east, and Scotland at 9.55am, and later trains ran to the Midlands, the north-west via Crewe, South Wales and London.

From Southampton, produce from the Channel Isles was marshalled in partially-fitted or fully-fitted freight trains running to 'Q' paths (as required) that were set out in the working timetable. The semi-fitted trains ran to Feltham, Nine Elms, Salisbury and Basingstoke, and fully-fitted ones ran to either Woodford Halse or Crewe over the DN&SR line, or via Basingstoke and Reading.

These trains from Southampton could include a variety of cargoes within the same train such as a van of Jersey potatoes next to one of citrus fruits from South Africa, the motive power being provided by either Eastleigh of Feltham shed. Then there was the banana traffic, where on one day in November 1958, after the banana boat arrived at

At the quayside at Weymouth on an unknown date, a consignment of tomatoes from Guernsey is seen being loaded into a 12ton ventilated van, the tomatoes having arrived on the *SS Sambur*. In 1940 this ship came under fire when evacuating troops. After 1948 it operated from both Southampton and Weymouth to and from the Channel Isles, but in May 1964 it was laid-up at Southampton prior to being sold to a Dutch firm of breakers. C.L. Caddy Collection

Southampton, 523 wagons in twelve trains left Southampton conveying bananas, probably from Jamaica, and with produce from South Africa and the Channel Isles.

In the 1950s, a four-week period during the perishables season averaged around 2,000 wagons of tomatoes each from Southampton and Weymouth, with 80 to 90 wagons dispatched daily. However, in the 1960s the perishables traffic of Jersey tomatoes and potatoes declined, but tomatoes arriving at Weymouth from Guernsey increased, due to the fact that, by 1963, BR ceased to deal with this traffic at Southampton. In 1964, BR increased its cartage rates by 40%, resulting in the loss of half the Guernsey fruit and vegetables to Shoreham. From the early 1970s the Channel Isles lost out to Holland, as they were unable to compete with the Dutch tomato supplies on price.

Steam-hauled perishables traffic continued on until the end of steam on the Southern Region in the summer of 1967, and on 18 June and again on 25 June 1967 Light Pacific No 34102 worked to Westbury from Weymouth with a train-load of tomatoes. Three other perishables workings from Weymouth were seen on 9 July 1967 — the last day of steam on the Southern Region. In 1973, perishables traffic from the Channel Isles to the port of Weymouth, including flowers, was lost to road haulage. The final cargo of tomatoes arrived at Weymouth from Guernsey in 1987, and from 1999 round tomatoes had ceased to be a commercial crop for the growers in Guernsey who then exported just specialist tomatoes.

At Empress Dock at Southampton, bananas from the West Indies are seen being unloaded from the ship in the early 1950s. The scene clearly shows the elevator conveyors, with the bunches of bananas secured in canvas pockets. After being unloaded from the ship the bananas would be passed along a horizontal conveyor alongside awaiting vans, which in cold weather would already be steam-heated before loading took place. Straw mattresses would be placed in the doorways of the vans to avoid damage to the bananas. Associated British Ports

A Bournemouth-allocated Southern 'King Arthur' class 4-6-0, No 30772 Sir Percivale, is pictured in March 1960 with an up banana special from Southampton Docks passing the signal box at Worting Junction, just west of Basingstoke. The two white disc headcode on the locomotive suggests that the train is bound for Nine Elms and routed via Woking, Chertsey, and Brentford. Derek Cross

Perishable traffic and flowers arriving from the Channel Isles at Weymouth would regularly commence their journey over Southern metals and then pass on to Western Region destinations like the train pictured here. The 15.06 perishables train of box vans, on 2 July 1967, during the final month of steam haulage on the Southern Region, is seen near Upway Wishing Well Halt, climbing towards Bincombe tunnel which is just five miles out from Weymouth. The train is being hauled by rebuilt 'West Country' Southern Light Pacific No 34021, now devoid of its *Dartmoor* nameplates, and is heading for Westbury. The climb to Bincombe tunnel from Weymouth ranges from 1 in 50 to 1 in 74, and the perishables special is seen being banked by another 'West Country' class Light Pacific, No 34093, also now devoid of its *Saunton* nameplates. Colour-Rail BRS27

The Maunsell 'W' class 2-6-4Ts were synonymous with cross-London goods traffic, but in later years they picked up a morning turn to Oxted yard. At around 9.00am on Saturday, 1 June 1963 we find 'W' class tank No 31920 in the sidings at Lingfield with a Fyffes banana special. After World War II huge quantities of bananas were imported in refrigerated ships from Jamaica, the West Indies, and the Windward Islands. To bring them to market they needed to ripen, and after the war Fyffes set up sheds for that purpose at East Croydon and Lingfield, enlisting the railway to assist by steam-heating the wagons from the port, although that practice had been dropped by the time rail traffic ceased in 1979. David Clark

A certain amount of the banana traffic from Southampton Docks commenced their journey over Southern Region metals but continued their journeys into other BR territory, such as the banana special pictured here. Still being hauled by a Southern Pacific locomotive, 'West Country' class rebuilt Light Pacific No 34100 *Appledore,* on 3 August 1965, the train is seen on the Western Region nearing Kidderminster, the bananas probably destined for Crewe. These trains were routed via the Oxford to Worcester line, Stourbridge Junction, and Wolverhampton. *Brian Moone*

Milk from the West Country to London

From 1942 the Milk Marketing Board controlled movement of all milk traffic, but by the late 1960s, apart from traffic destined for Express Dairies and Unigate (a company formed by the merger of United Dairies and Cow & Gate), all the milk from the West Country went by road. Milk from the West Country travelled by rail up over Southern metals on a daily basis to the United Dairies creamery and bottling plant at Vauxhall, and to the Express Dairies creamery at Morden South to be pasteurised and processed. The Morden South plant had opened in March 1954 and remained open until the early 1980s.

Loaded milk tanks were assembled at road-served loading points at Torrington, Seaton Junction, Chard Junction, and Semley,

Pictured at 8.04pm on Bank Holiday Monday, 18 May 1964, the 6.15pm Axminster to London milk train, heads east as it breasts the summit of the 1 in 80 incline from Sherborne on the Exeter to Salisbury line, and approaches Milborne Port, hauled by rebuilt 'Battle of Britain' Pacific No 34059 *Sir Archibald Sinclair.* At Clapham Junction the loaded milk train will be split, some loaded milk tanks heading for the bottling plant at Vauxhall, and others going to the Morden South dairy. *M. Mensing*

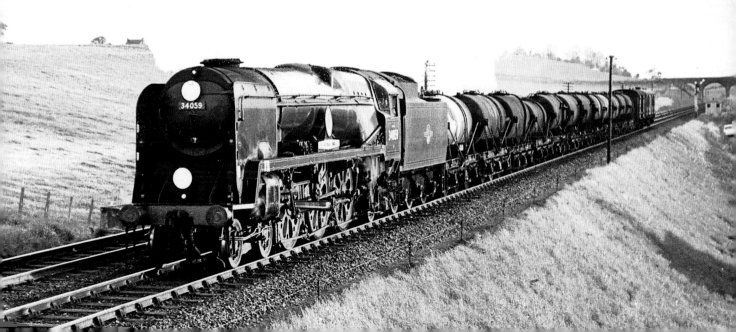

The transportation of milk shifted from churns to glass-lined tankers, and so in the late 1940s a bespoke milk depot was constructed at the back of the goods shed at Torrington. As seen here, overhead pipework was installed above the siding to feed the milk into rail wagons, which was brought up from the nearby Cow & Gate creamery by road. A concrete drain between the rails dealt with spillage. In this early 1960s view a pair of Ivatt '2P' 2-6-2Ts are busy in the station area marshalling passenger coaches, all services from both the Barnstaple direction and Halwill terminated at Torrington. The Halwill services ran as mixed trains, with just a single coach and goods wagons as required conveyed. Through carriages for Waterloo and milk tank wagons were conveyed on trains towards Barnstaple. J. Nicholas Collection

Bottom: **On 11 June 1962, in this interesting busy scene at Seaton Junction, Salisbury-based 'S15' 4-6-0 No 30823 pulls out of the yard in the early evening with a train of grimy-looking milk tanks for Clapham Junction, subsequently destined for the Express Dairy plant at Morden South and the United Dairies creamery and bottling plant at Vauxhall. Seaton Junction was one of the locations where the tank wagons were filled with milk for their journey up to London and, as can be seen from the amount of milk tanks on view, was a busy location for these daily milk trains.** Peter W. Gray

with Lapford, Yeovil Town, and Bailey Gate (on the S&DJR) feeding into the traffic flow. The Torrington milk tanks were split, due to weight, and conveyed as far as Barnstaple Junction on the rear of passenger trains, with eight being despatched on the 2.52pm train, and a further six were added to the 4.37pm departure in the 1962 Summer Timetable period, for instance. At Barnstaple, milk tanks were attached to Ilfracombe line trains, with the first tank wagons detached at Crediton,

where they were joined by milk traffic from Lapford before onward movement to London. Another train gained traffic at Seaton Junction and Chard Junction before feeder services from Yeovil Town and Bailey Gate were added at Templecombe. Semley was the final collection point, with arrival in London in the early hours.

At Clapham Junction the train would be split in two for unloading in the Windsor line up platform at Vauxhall where a pipe would

discharge the milk through a subway under the running lines and across the road to the United Dairies creamery on the south side. The empty tanks would return to Clapham Junction via a turn-over engine at Waterloo, and the second half of the load would be picked up and the same procedure would again take place at Vauxhall.

The Express Dairy plant at Morden South had a small yard of three sidings at its milk bottling plant situated on the down side of the

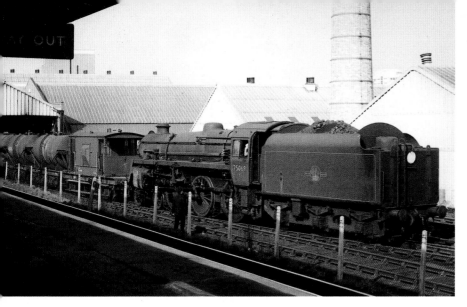

A view of the sidings that served the Express Dairy plant at Morden South where full milk tanks would arrive from Clapham Junction in the early hours of the morning, having travelled up from the West Country. On the occasion pictured here, BR Riddles '4MT' 4-6-0 No 75069 is seen shunting empty milk tanks in the Express Dairy yard, an engine of the class allocated to Nine Elms shed from August 1963 to May 1965. Alistair Nisbet

On leaving the Express Dairy at Morden South, after picking up the empty milk tanks for Clapham Junction yard in the early afternoon, the train of empties would join the South Western main line at Wimbledon West Junction, where the illustrated empties train is pictured. In charge of the train on 30 May 1965 is BR '4MT' 4-6-0 No 75078 with the 13.07 train from St. Helier, near to the Morden South bottling plant. Sometimes a 'Q1' 0-6-0 was delegated this duty. A. Wooller

Any available motive power was sent from Nine Elms shed to collect the empty milk tanks from the Morden South bottling plant to return them to Clapham Junction yard for eventual return to the West Country. In August 1962 we see a Southern 'S15' class 4-6-0, No 30839, allocated to this duty as it passes through Clapham Junction station with the milk empties. The train is seen passing Southern 'U1' class Mogul No 31909, which is in the Windsor line platform at the station. F. Hornby/Colour-Rail 91298

At Clapham Junction on 2 June 1956 former Southern 'N15' class Urie 'King Arthur' 4-6-0, No 30751 *Etarre*, waits to shunt the train of milk empties seen ahead of it, which is hauled by ex-L&SWR 'M7' class 0-4-4T No 30320, that have arrived at Clapham Junction for eventually return to the West Country.
P.J. Lynch/Kidderminster Railway Museum 093438

An unrebuilt 'West Country class Pacific, No 34108 *Wincanton,* is pictured in 1960 passing through Wimbledon park station with returning milk empties for Exeter and the West Country, a train which left mid-afternoon from Clapham Junction yard. Note that the Pacific locomotive is fitted with a cut-down tender. Lens of Sutton Collection

former LB&SCR line from Wimbledon to Sutton. Here also, the milk arriving at the plant was discharged by the use of a pipeline, and trains of milk tanks would arrive in the early hours of the morning. The locomotive would then run a few yards down the line to St. Helier to cross over to the up line and return light-engine to Wimbledon West yard. A locomotive would then go down light to

Unrebuilt Southern 'Battle of Britain' class Pacific No 34086 *219 Squadron* is pictured here with the 3.35pm Clapham Junction to Exeter milk empties having just passed East Putney on 11 July 1964, the train including some empty milk tanks from the Express Dairy at Morden South. The train is running over the tracks shared with London Transport's District Line services towards Wimbledon. The line has now been transferred to London Transport control, and is correspondingly resignalled to their standards, rather than BR Southern Region ones. Brian Stephenson

Passing through Wimbledon on the South Western main line are the returning empty milk tanks that would have arrived in London full for the Express dairy at Morden South and the United Dairies bottling plant at Vauxhall. The train of empties is seen hauled by Southern 'Merchant Navy' Pacific No 35027 *Port Line* on 9 July 1964, an engine of the class saved from the cutter's torch. It was not unusual to see a locomotive of this class on this duty. K. Fairey/Colour-Rail 18793

recover the empty tanks in the afternoon and take them up to Clapham Junction yard. The motive power for this duty was usually a 'Q1' 0-6-0 until the early 1960s, although after this time any available locomotive was used, including BR 2-6-4Ts and 2-6-2Ts to 4-6-0s.

At Clapham Junction yard the empty milk tanks would be joined by other empty tank wagons for the West Country from Vauxhall,

and returned west. In the Summer 1962 Timetable this train ran as the 3.54pm to Exeter Central via East Putney (4.00pm on Saturdays, and 3.50pm on Sunday)

Over the years a variety of motive power could be seen on the milk trains to and from the West Country from Southern Pacific locomotives (both unrebuilt and rebuilt versions) to Southern 'S15' class 4-6-0s.

The Surbiton to Okehampton car-carrier trains

The holiday resorts of Devon and Cornwall have always been favourite English locations for a summer break, but as more and more people acquired cars, roads through Honiton and around Exeter, in particular, became huge bottlenecks, and one could literally spend hours sat in traffic. However, if you were travelling

After passing through Basingstoke station on 1 August 1964, and signalled for the Salisbury line at Worting Junction, returning milk tanks for the West Country pass under the signal gantry where the line for Salisbury leaves the South Western main line to Southampton and Bournemouth. In charge of the train is rebuilt 'Battle of Britain' Pacific No 34058 *Sir Frederick Pile*, an engine of the class allocated to Eastleigh at this time. Colour-Rail 7826

At the starting point at the London end for the car-carrier trains to Okehampton on 8 July 1960, Nine Elms-allocated rebuilt 'Merchant Navy Pacific No 35029 *Ellerman Lines* awaits departure for the West Country from the bay at Surbiton station. This was during the second month that these trains first operated. From Exeter to Okehampton a Light Pacific generally hauled the train. The return trip to Surbiton on this occasion was hauled by sister locomotive No 35001 *Channel Packet*.

Illustrated is the situation that the car-carrier trains to the West Country avoided for travelling holidaymakers. When these trains were introduced in 1960 the Southern Region produced posters advertising the service which were displayed at a variety of stations, like the one pictured here showing traffic jams in Topsham Road, Exeter — a regular bottleneck. Railwaymen are seen walking alongside the queues of cars, trying to encourage the drivers to use the railway's new carrier-car service.
F. Collins/Courtesy Silver Link Publishing Ltd

On Summer Saturdays in 1961, the car-carrier trains from Surbiton to Okehampton became so popular that an additional van was added to the train, to now convey 24 vehicles, and the service was extended to run on Summer Fridays, Saturdays, and Sundays. The train pictured here on Saturday, 29 July 1961, hauled by 'Merchant Navy' Pacific No 35017 *Belgian Marine,* is seen with eight green-liveried GUVs and a restaurant car as it passes Fox Hills, west of Brookwood in Surrey. Alan Dixon

DAY CAR/CARRIER SERVICE
SURBITON—OKEHAMPTON : SATURDAYS

		SATURDAYS 30th May, 6th June, 13th June and 12th September	SATURDAYS 20th June to 5th September, inclusive
Surbiton	..dep	8 03 am	8 03 am
Okehampton	arr	12 28 pm	12 26 pm
Okehampton	dep	3 08 pm	3 55 pm
Surbiton	..arr	7 15 pm	8 11 pm

Fares *

		Single	Return
Driver and Car	.. .. ..£	10 10 0	£17 0 0
Additional Passengers	2 6 6	4 13 0
Children age 3 and under 14	1 3 3	2 6 6

* A Peak Surcharge is made on outward journeys from 25th July to 29th August inclusive - Driver and Car £1 10 0 single £3 0 0 return.

WATERLOO—EXETER (CENTRAL) : SUNDAYS

SUNDAYS: 31st May to 6th September, inclusive
Waterloo .. dep 9 00 am
Exeter Central arr 12 50 pm

SUNDAYS: 31st May to 13th September, inclusive
Exeter Central dep 4 12 pm
Waterloo .. arr 7 49 pm

Fares

		Single	Return
Driver and Car	.. .. ..£	9 10 0	£15 0 0
Additional Passengers	2 3 0	4 6 0
Children age 3 and under 14	1 1 6	2 3 0

For reservations and further information apply to the Line Manager, South Western Division, 19 Worple Road, Wimbledon, S.W.19.

A timetable detailing the timings and fare structure for the car-carrier trains.

Southern 'Merchant Navy' Pacific No 35001 *Channel Packet* cruises into Exeter (Central) station with the car-carrier train from Surbiton on 20 August 1960, during the first years of the train's operation. The carriage boards carried by these trains are clearly visible. There would be a change of motive power at Exeter, usually to a Light Pacific, for the last part of the journey to Okehampton due to weight restrictions west of Exeter. M.J. Fox/Rail Archive Stephenson

from the London area there was a solution provided by the Southern Region of British Railways from 18 June 1960 to 12 September 1964 in the summer timetable — the car-carrier train from Surbiton in the London suburbs to Okehampton in Devon, conveying both family and car to the West Country.

The formation of these car-carrier trains on the Southern Region included three carriages for passengers comprising a Bulleid brake second open, a Bulleid kitchen/restaurant car (except in the first year

of operation), and a BR Mk I second open, and eight GUV utility vans, each van carrying three cars. Trains left Surbiton from the carriage dock where the cars were loaded, and the train for Okehampton via Salisbury left at 8.03am for its 4½-hour journey. The train was Nine Elms duty No 8, rostered for a 'Merchant Navy' Pacific, although Light Pacifics were also used at times. A second-class return fare of £12 for driver and car was at first levied, plus an additional supplement for any other passengers.

The train's very first run to Okehampton on 18 June 1960 was worked by 'Merchant Navy' Pacific No 35029 *Ellerman Lines,* and Light Pacific No 34023 *Blackmore Vale* took over the train at Exeter to complete the journey to Okehampton, and it also worked the return trip to Exeter. The returning train from Exeter to Surbiton was hauled by 'Battle of Britain' Pacific No 34050 *Royal Observer Corps.*

On arrival at Okehampton at 12.28pm the Okehampton station pilot, possibly a former

A view of the Military sidings at Okehampton, where cars were unloaded from the car-carrier trains after their arrival from Surbiton in Surrey. The vehicles from one of these trains is seen on the left with the rear doors open in readiness for the cars of returning holidaymakers to London. Passing the sidings on 29 August 1964, during the final years for the car-carrier trains, is Southern 'N' class Mogul No 31845 on a North Cornwall line service, probably for Padstow. Colour-Rail 341498

L&SWR 'T9' 4-4-0 or a 'N' class Mogul, backed on to the rear of the train then, after the train engine had been detached, hauled the carriages and vans into the Military sidings, a short distance from the station, where passengers alighted and cars were unloaded.

After loading with returning holiday-makers from the West Country the train for Surbiton left at 3.55pm, just 3½ hours after it had arrived, and it was scheduled to arrive at Surbiton at 8.11pm, holiday-makers thankful that they had not had to queue in long traffic jams but were able to relax, travelling with their cars by train to and from Okehampton. On arrival at Surbiton a Guildford-allocated Mogul would shunt the vans down the yard for unloading, and the carriages would proceed up to Clapham yard for servicing. For the following 1961 season the return fare was increased to £15 for car and driver, with £3 for any additional passenger.

As most people took their holidays from Saturday to Saturday, most of the Sunday services were soon cancelled due to lack of patronage, some just running with a few cars on board. It was then decided that in cases where only a few cars with their families wanted to use the service, one or two vans were attached to the 9.00am train from Waterloo, returning on the 4.12pm train. The same situation occurred on Fridays when patronage was low.

The last car-carrier train from Surbiton to Okehampton ran in 1964 as although the return fare for car and driver had increased to £20, British Railways hardly broke even when it came to running costs, and less holiday-makers were taking advantage of this service due to improved road schemes such as the Honiton by-pass, and more and more people were taking holidays abroad. The Exeter M5 motorway by-pass was not completed until 1977, and the Okehampton A30 one in 1988. The car-carrier Military sidings at Oakhampton were taken out of use in November 1982. The car-carrier train remained predominantly steam-hauled to the end, out-living the steam-hauled 'Atlantic Coast Express' by one week. Okehampton lost its normal passenger services in 1972.

Hop-pickers trains

The hop-picking season in England started in September each year, the main area of the country on the Southern Region for hop-growing being Kent, where the Southern Railway and, later, the Southern Region of British Railways laid on regular trains of pickers to harvest this important crop. As far back as the 1870s 70,000 acres of hops were grown, bit this reduced to 10,000 acres in Kent by the mid-1930s. Most pickers that took advantage of the hop-pickers trains to Kent came from the London area and were chiefly women and children who during their stay working in the hop fields were provided with accommodation in farms. Some of these families would return each year, some carrying out this hard working task for over ten years, and it was certainly hard work. Needless to say, the local public houses were well patronized, some remaining open until midnight resulting, at times, in fighting amongst the 'hoppers'.

For the hop-pickers trains, the Southern Railway and later the Southern Region of BR, put in place a temporary operational centre at

A returning car-carrier trains from Okehampton is pictured here at Seaton Junction on 13 May 1963, hauled by named BR '5MT' 4-6-0 No 73086 *The Green Knight* and piloted by the now-preserved unrebuilt 'West Country' Pacific No 34092 *City of Wells* of Salisbury shed. Generally, east of Exeter for these trains, a 'Merchant Navy' Pacific would be in charge of the train. David Anderson

A hop-pickers special train in Southern Railway days, pictured on 6 September 1934 at Tonbridge in Kent. The locomotive is seen hauling the very old third class six-wheeled stock that was used on these trains at that time, and that contained no lavatories. Carrying the reporting number 107, the train is being hauled by former S&ECR 'C' class 0-6-0 No 1725. The station platform is concrete-faced, and the station's running-in board is on the right. V.R. Websyer/Kidderminster Railway Museum 016905

Paddock Wood, and hop-pickers 'friends' trains were also run for relatives who wished to visit the hop-pickers at weekends at their temporary accommodation. The rolling stock for the hop-pickers and hop-pickers friends train generally comprised the oldest third-class-only carriages without lavatories.

The first hop-pickers trains were SER trains from Bricklayers Arms, but this was soon to change to the low-level platforms at London Bridge, and hop-pickers would arrive up to four hours prior to their trains'

departure, sometimes with crying children, prams, and barrows, waiting for the booking office to open. In those early years these trains would make a call at New Cross, and sometimes at Grove Park on their way to the Kent hop-fields. On reaching Paddock Wood, in the centre of the growing area, trains then called at Marden, Staplehurst, Headcorn and Pluckley stations, and another heavy hop-growing area was the district around the Hawkhurst branch, with stations covered being Horsmonden, Goudhurst, and

Cranbrook. The other area covered by the trains was around Selling on the Faversham to Canterbury line and there were also hop fields served by the Kent & East Sussex Railway.

To show just how popular these trains were and the increased revenue generated by the Southern Railway, in the 1935 season the SR ran 40 outward trains conveying 15,227 'hoppers' and 42 homebound trains, and 33.000 hop-pickers friends travelled by trains to and from the fields. As will be seen from the Illustrations here, some of these trains were very long, and

In early BR days, in October 1949, a Wainwright 'E' class 4-4-0, No S1491, with the BRITISH RAILWAYS lettering on its tender, is pictured at Penshurst on the former S&ECR line between Edenbridge and Tonbridge in Kent, with a hop pickers' special from London Bridge (Low Level) to Paddock Wood via Oxted and the Crowhurst spur. K.W. Wightman

On Sunday, 14 September 1952 the 6.05pm homeward-bound hop pickers' friends special is seen at Northiam on the Kent & East Sussex Railway prior to departing for Bodiam and Junction Road, and then on to London Road station. 'Terrier' 0-6-0T No 32659 is bunker-first at the front of the train and sister locomotive No 32678 is at the rear. On reaching Robertsbridge these two locomotives will pass the train over to a tender engine. As this is a hop pickers' friends train, the luggage accommodation in the two Maunsell Hastings-gauge 3-car sets, Nos 213 and 215, will be more than adequate. Neil Sprinks

London Bridge (Low Level) station was the starting point from the city of London for the hop-pickers and their friends' trains, and on 3 September 1955 a hop pickers' special waits in the platform at this station in preparation to depart for the hop fields in Kent. Hauling this train is Southern 'Schools' class 4-4-0 No 30913 *Christ's Hospital* which is carrying the reporting number H67.
G. Siviour/Kidderminster Railway Museum 165882

On 14 September 1957 at Robertsbridge, during the hop-picking season, near to the former Kent & East Sussex line, in the bay platform is an 'A1X' class 'Terrier' 0-6-0T, No 32678, at the head of two 100-seater former SE&CR compartment coaches and an SR 4-wheeled brake. These steam-hauled specials, apart from providing a connection with main line services, ran on Saturdays so that hop-pickers could go to Robertsbridge to purchase food. E. Wilmshurst

A variety of motive power was used for hop-pickers trains over the years, from 'Terrier' tanks and 'C' class 0-6-0s to 'D1', 'E', 'L' and 'Schools' class 4-4-0s and, on occasions, even an LMS Fairburn 2-6-4T was used. In this 1958 scene at Paddock Wood station a London Bridge to Maidstone West hop pickers' special is seen being hauled by a former SE&CR 'D1' class 4-4-0, No 31735. Paddock Wood was the operational centre for the hop-pickers trains. G. Siviour/Kidderminster Railway Museum 166058

because 'hoppers' brought prams and carts along, up to four PMV vans were included in the trains to accommodate this extra 'luggage'.

In Southern Railway days during the 1943 picking season seventeen trains left London Bridge on weekdays, one from New Cross, and one from Woolwich Arsenal. On Sunday, 31 August 1947 three 'friends' trains ran to Paddock Wood for the Hawkhurst branch and seven return trains worked up to London — some 'friends' stayed overnight with their relatives in the fields.

During the 1950s in BR days more modern rolling stock was used on these trains, some being corridor coaches from other BR regions. In these BR days the motive power for the hop-pickers and friends trains would be a 0-6-0 goods locomotive, a 4-4-0, a Maunsell Mogul, or a BR '4MT' 2-6-4T, but on the Hawkhurst branch the Moguls were barred, as were 2-6-4Ts and 'L' and 'L1' class 4-4-0s.

The decline of the hop-pickers trains came in the mid to late 1950s when harvesting machines were more used that had been introduced in the late 1940s. However, in the 1957 season there were still ten hop-pickers trains booked, but some trains were cancelled during the 1958 season due to freak storms and serious flooding in the hop fields, but twelve 'friends' trains still ran that year, some hauled by 'Schools' class 4-4-0s. Due to mechanized picking of the hops, the last 'pickers' trains ran in September 1960, and soon after this the Hawkhurst branch was closed to traffic.

In September 1959, the last through returning train of the hop-picking season from Hawkhurst to London Bridge stands in the station at Cranbrook, the penultimate station down the branch. Hauling the train is former SE&CR 'C' class 0-6-0 No 31293 carrying the reporting number H84. The hop-fields were prolific near the Hawkhurst branch with Horsmonden, Goudhurst, Cranbrook, and Hawkhurst all being served by the hop-pickers trains. G. Siviour/Kidderminster Railway Museum 165900

In the final season for the hop-pickers trains, 1960, former SE&CR Wainwright 'C' class 0-6-0 No 31588 leaves Paddock Wood, the nerve centre for the hop-picking specials, in October of that year with a hop-pickers train, comprising red-liveried coaching stock. The leading vehicle in the train is an ex-SE&CR composite with a saloon section. After 1960 the mechanized picking of the hops resulted in the end of the hop-pickers trains — until then a main feature of Kent's railways. D. Cross/Colour-Rail BRS112

Most of the information provided in this article on 'Special traffic on the Southern' has been taken from the late Michael Harris's extensive notes for the perishables and hop-pickers trains, most of which were published in greater detail in the June 1999 and July and December issues of STEAM DAYS magazine, and for the Morden South milk traffic from Alistair Nisbet's article in the October 2003 issue.

My thanks must also go to Roger Smith for his extensive research regarding milk traffic from 1962 working timetables.

Information provided for the car-carrier trains are from Jeffery Grayer's article that appeared in more detail in the May 2003 issue of STEAM DAYS magazine, all of these articles mentioned providing far more detailed information.

Passing through Wateringbury station on the former SE&CR line from Maidstone to Paddock Wood, deep into Kent's hop-growing country, former SE&CR 'C' class 0-6-0 No 31273 hauls a long hop-pickers train of the period, identifiable by the reporting number H70 on the engine's smokebox door. Derek Cross

THE GREAT ELECTRIC TRAIN SHOW

SAVE ON THE ENTRY PRICE WHEN YOU BOOK ADVANCE TICKETS TODAY!

BRITISH MOTOR MUSEUM, WARWICKSHIRE CV35 0BJ

Bere Banks - 'OO' Gauge

SAVE £s WHEN BOOKING IN ADVANCE

ADULT £9 Save £3*
CHILD (5-16 yrs) **£7** Save £2*

Children under 16 must be accompanied by an adult at all times. *Savings against BMM on-the-day ticket prices. Deadline for advance ticket orders 29 September 2017.

OCTOBER 7/8 2017
25+ WORKING LAYOUTS
in the major scales, gauges and eras, including:

- **Bere Banks** - 'OO', Western Region, 1970s
- **Kingsbury** - 'O', Great Western, 1930s
- **Rannoch Moor** - 'OO', Scottish Region, 2000s
- **Tedburn St Mary** - 'OO', Great Western, 1930s
- **Twelve Trees Junction** - 'OO', Southern Region, 1960s

Practical demonstrations for hands-on advice and inspiration as well as a wide selection of top quality traders and manufacturers

TICKET PRICE WILL INCLUDE:
- FREE ACCESS TO BRITISH MOTOR MUSEUM
- FREE ON-SITE PARKING
- FREE COURTESY BUS FROM LEAMINGTON SPA TRAIN STATION (Saturday Only)

Check website for full list of layouts, demonstrations and exhibitors

220/17

Advance ticket holders: Express lanes in operation. Entry from 9.30am.
Opening times: Saturday October 7: 10am to 5pm
AND **Sunday October 8:** 10am to 4pm.

To purchase advance tickets visit:
www.greatelectrictrainshow.com
or call: 01780 480 404

Brought to you by

ON THE DAY PRICES:
- Adult: £12
- Child (5-16 yrs): £9
- Children under 5: FREE

Fawley oil traffic

Rex Kennedy takes a brief look at the workings of oil trains from Fawley's oil refinery in Hampshire, and the variety of motive power used to haul these trains of oil tanks.

Prior to the massive expansion of the Esso Refinery at Fawley in the early 1950s, oil traffic from the small installation on the western bank of the River Test estuary on the Southern Railway-built Fawley branch was handled by a variety of former LB&SCR 'E4' and 'E6' class 0-6-2Ts, together with the Maunsell 'Z' class 0-8-0 shunting tanks. Curiously, these big tanks had an LB&SCR connection as their boilers were an adaption of the LB&SCR Marsh 'C3' class 0-6-0 boiler. Sporting the earliest BRITISH RAILWAYS lettering in Southern Railway style, 'Z' class 0-8-0T No 30956 is seen passing through Southampton (Central) station with the 1.30pm Northam yard to Fawley freight train, including empty oil tanks, in December 1950. J.B. Hayman

From Southern Railway days, the Fawley branch in Hampshire saw many trains of oil tanks, to and from the oil refining and storage facilities on Southampton Water, and in 1951 a new Esso refinery was opened at Fawley, increasing the oil traffic over the line. At this time BR and Ivatt 2-6-2Ts seemed to be the order of the day for these trains, replacing former LB&SCR 'E4' and 'E6' class 0-6-2Ts and 'Z' class 0-8-0Ts often working in tandem, depending on the length of the train of tank wagons.

By the early 1960s, Britain was experiencing something of an oil boom as it became a cheap alternative to coal, not only for industrial use but also for domestic central heating. Huge oil tankers brought crude oil to oil refineries such as Fawley, so the railways were able to participate in the oil boom by transporting the refined oil by rail throughout Britain.

On 2 December 1963 the largest single train-load of petroleum products, in 54 vacuum-braked oil tank wagons, ever to run in BR days left Fawley *en route* for Bromford, on the outskirts of Birmingham, travelling at a speed of 60mph. The train was 500yds long and carried 1,000tons of oil. Similar trains were soon to run at a rate of five per week, all due to a contract signed between British Railways and the Esso Petroleum Company. These trains carried 1,000tons of petroleum products, including petrol, diesel oil, and paraffin, with a 'gross' weight of 2,000tons. On occasions these limits were exceeded, as on 17 February 1964 when an extra-long oil train left Fawley double-headed by a BR Standard '3MT' 2-6-2T and a BRCW 'Type 3' Bo-Bo diesel locomotive.

The increasing weight of the bulk oil trains in 1960s brought more variety of

The BR '3MT' Standard 2-6-2Ts became the staple power on the oil trains in the mid and late 1950s, but by the end of the decade they were being outclassed. Dieselisation of the marshalling yards and traffic at Feltham led to the powerful Urie 'H16' class 4-6-2Ts used on the transfer workings around London becoming redundant, so in January 1960 'H16' No 30516 went to Eastleigh to assist the BR Standard engines and to undertake marshalling duties at Fawley itself. This engine was soon joined by the remaining engines of the class, and is seen on 23 February 1961 being piloted through Southampton (Central) by BR '3MT' 2-6-2T No 82016 on the 1.20pm oil tank train from Fawley to Bevois Park sidings which were on the up side of the main line near St. Denys. J.C. Haydon

Bottom left: The tank engines only worked trains along the Fawley branch to Totton and through Southampton (Central) to the marshalling yards just beyond the junction with the original London & Southampton Railway at Northam. There were separate up and down yards, Northam yard dealing with down traffic and, a mile or so up the line, Bevois Park the up traffic. Trains changed engines in these yards, tender locomotives bringing empties down from the Midlands and taking loaded trains north. A Maunsell 'U' class Mogul, No 31794, is seen here on the former Great Western's Didcot, Newbury & Southampton line at Highclere with southbound empties in April 1960. The Southern Region had acquired this line in the regional boundaries shuffles of 1950, and had just withdrawn all passenger services on it to enable it to become the main oil artery to the industrial areas of the Midlands. The 'U' class 2-6-0 itself was built as an express passenger engine of the 'River' class, so was not really a suitable type for freight traffic, but was used as such in Hampshire as the 'N' class Moguls, designated as mixed traffic engines, were not allocated to this area at all.

Below: The Fawley branch was upgraded in 1960 to allow heavier and longer oil trains to be worked, the loops at Marchwood being doubled in length with effect from 31 July of that year, so this became the main passing place on the line. Shortly before this, 'H16' class 4-6-2T No 30516 is again seen, this time working solo on a train of oil tank empties to Fawley at Trott's Lane Crossing on 12 May 1961, a mile from the new loop. The line had been built under the provisions of the Light Railways Act of 1896, so there were numerous ungated level crossings on the route, and speeds were restricted to 25 miles per hour. J.C. Haydon

motive power for these trains as in 1960 when Urie 'H16' class 4-6-2T No 30516 was tested over the Fawley branch, although this freight locomotive was soon to be replaced by the equally-massive Maunsell 'W' class 2-6-4Ts, such as Nos 31912, 31917, and 31922, all alloated to Eastleigh shed at this time. By the mid-1960s two oil trains were booked to leave Fawley each day, and on 15 April 1965 one of these trains was unusually hauled by former GWR 2-8-0s Nos 3837 and 3854.

The first true block oil train made of a dedicated stock, comprising twenty tank wagons, left Fawley for Spondon, near Derby, in September 1960, the returning empties working to Eastleigh being hauled by 'Modified Hall' No 6991 Acton Burnell Hall. The running of the oil trains from Fawley to Bromford Bridge, near Birmingham, did not commence until October 1960, changing locomotives at Millbrook yard, and then running via Eastleigh, Chandlers Ford, Salisbury and Bristol to Birmingham. In December of that year the Western Region loaned three BR '9F' 2-10-0s, Nos 92205, 92206, and 92231 to Eastleigh to work the oil trains from Fawley, avoiding a change of motive power at Westbury. These 2-10-0s were later increased to five with the arrival at Eastleigh of Nos 92211 and 92239, but many other engines of the class, allocated to a variety of sheds, were seen on the oil trains in later days.

Delays were being experienced in the Bristol area at times, and this resulted in re-routing the oil trains over the Didcot, Newbury & Southampton Railway line which had closed to passenger in March 1960, the oil trains using this route from January 1961. During the early 1960s a variety of motive power was seen on the Fawley oil trains such as Stanier '8F' 2-8-0s Nos 48635 and 48669 on Northampton-bound trains. WD 'Austerity' 2-8-0s would also appear, as would 'Black Fives' and even LMS 'Jubilees', but probably the most unexpected arrival from Bromford Bridge with empties in June 1961 was ex-LMS 'Patriot' No 45509 Royal Pioneer Corps and even a 'Royal Scot' 4-6-0 in March 1962.

Due to a derailment of a BR Standard '9F' 2-10-0-hauled Fawley to Bromford oil train on the Didcot, Newbury and Southampton line on 14 October 1961 at Worthy Down, this resulted in the oil trains being diverted through Basingstoke and Reading; another derailment, involving 22 oil tanks, happened on the DN&S line on 23 March 1964.

Eventually as the diesel era emerged, Birmingham Railway & Carriage Works 'Type 3' diesels took over some of the Fawley oil trains in 1962, and in 1963 new long-term agreements were signed between British

Unfortunately the 'H16' 4-6-2Ts were virtually worn out before they were transferred to Southampton, so in June 1961 five Maunsell 'W' class 2-6-4Ts were transferred to Eastleigh to take their place, the five 'H16s' returning to Feltham from where they were all withdrawn by the end of 1962. The 'W' class engines were tank versions of the 'N' class Moguls and incorporated the tanks and bunkers from the original 'River' class engines which had been converted into 'U' class Moguls. Because of the history of the 'River' class locomotives the 'W' class 2-6-4Ts were banned from passenger work, but were much more suitable for the oil trains than the passenger engines, and here we see No 31922 of that class working with BR '3MT' 2-6-2T No 82016, unusually heading oil tanks south through Eastleigh station on the down fast line on 25 March 1962. Colour-Rail BRS846

During the 1960s various 'foreign' locomotives were to be seen on Southern metals as dieselisation made many classes obsolete, and thus available to work all sorts of traffic. Most were former LMS engines as most of the traffic worked to locations on the London Midland Region. On 14 February 1961 a Stanier '8F' 2-8-0 is seen with the 2.20pm Esso train to Bromford Bridge, near Castle Bromwich in Birmingham on the Birmingham to Derby main line, as it runs into Southampton. These trains changed engines in Millbrook yard, a short distance to the west of Southampton (Central). J.C. Haydon

Perhaps one of the strangest sights was to see a former LMS rebuilt 'Royal Scot' on an oil train! On 7 March 1962 No 46122 *Royal Ulster Rifleman* is seen heading north through Southampton (Central) on the 10.25am Fawley to Bromford Bridge oil tanks. As before, it had taken over the train at Millbrook, these trains initially being routed via Eastleigh, Chandler's Ford, Romsey, Salisbury, Westbury, Bristol, and Bromsgrove to Birmingham. It was delays to these trains in the Bristol area that lead to the re-routing of many of them over the Didcot, Newbury & Southampton line following the cessation of passenger services over that route. J.C. Haydon

It seems that the London Midland Region was trying to find work for its locomotives as the 2.20pm working to Bromford Bridge is seen yet again at Southampton (Central) on 21 September 1961 behind another Stanier express locomotive, this time 'Jubilee' No 45682 *Kempenfelt* and, again, working through Southampton (Central) where normally tank engines reigned supreme. J.C. Haydon

Railways and the major oil companies for the transportation of petroleum products, using the oil company's own fleet of wagons, and this resulted in two hundred block trains of petroleum products per week in 1964, carrying 90,000 tons of oil products, and in April 1964 a new oil train service worked between Fawley and Hethersett in Norfolk, running via Staines and the North London line.

Taking the Chandler's Ford line at Eastleigh in August 1961 is another visiting London Midland Region-allocated locomotive, BR '9F' 2-10-0 No 92136, with a Bromford Bridge train comprising two barrier wagons and a string of the company-owned Class 'A' tank wagons which had been built in large numbers at the end of the 1950s for the expanding oil traffic. The barrier wagons were always marshalled between the locomotive and the first tank wagons for safety reasons. L Elsey/Colour-Rail BRS869

Obviously the logical type of locomotive for the heavy oil traffic was a pure freight engine, so with the London Midland Region visitors proving successful, a number of BR '9F' 2-10-0s were transferred from the Western Region to Eastleigh depot with effect from December 1960, all sporting the inset-bunker type BR1A tenders. No 92231 was one of the first three to be transferred, and is seen leaving the up loop at Allbrook, just north of Eastleigh, with a train which was scheduled to run via the Didcot, Newbury & Southampton line to Bromford Bridge on 25 May 1962. L. Elsey

The railway scene was changing rapidly in the early 1960s and the Didcot, Newbury & Southampton line's new status of being a major freight artery lasted barely three years; it was closed throughout on 4 August 1964. During that time its infrastructure had remained unchanged, with the exception of the demolition of station structures, so the freights still had to work under the old system of token working over the single-track sections. Here another London Midland Region BR '9F' 2-10-0, No 92137, is seen at the devastated Winchester (Chesil) station awaiting the token to proceed over the final single-line stretch from here to Shawford Junction on the Southampton main line. Platform 14 Collection MF1746

In the 1970s a great deal of the oil traffic by rail was lost to oil pipelines, coupled with the availability of North Sea Gas causing an oil crisis in 1973, resulting a reduction in rail-borne oil traffic. The last train of crude oil arrived at the Fawley refinery by rail from Holybourne, near Alton in Hampshire (the distribution point for the Hampshire oil field) on 4 September 2016, the train hauled by a 'Class 66' diesel locomotive, and the last oil trains to leave Fawley, containing diesel fuel for BR diesel depots left Fawley on 24 April 2015. The Red Dye plant at Fawley was deemed too expensive to refurbish and replace. A red dye was added to oil for commercial use, on which no duty was levied. The loss of the oil traffic was due to the spread of the National oil pipeline network and the changes in the way that tax was paid on fuel.

ACKNOWLEDGEMENTS

Stanley Jenkins, Roger Smith, and Jeffrey Grayer whose excellent fully-detailed article on the Fawley Oil Traffic appeared in the January 2005 issue of STEAM DAYS magazine

The boom in the oil traffic meant that it had become one of the major revenue earners on the Southern Region's Western Division, so the variety of steam locomotives was soon tempered by the availability of the region's 'Type 3' diesels (better known as the 'Class 33' Cromptons) from 1963 onwards as they took over from steam. Nevertheless, steam locomotives worked oil trains right up until the end of steam on the Southern, as witnessed by BR '5MT' 4-6-0 No 73029 on a Fawley-bound train passing the sidings at Millbrook on 5 January 1967. Note that the open barrier wagons had by now been replaced by brake vans at each end of the train. Tank wagons are seen in the sidings, where the trains had exchanged tanks engines for tender locomotives for the Bromford Bridge traffic, the engine pictured here probably being exchanged at Totton. John H. Bird/Platform 14 G5213

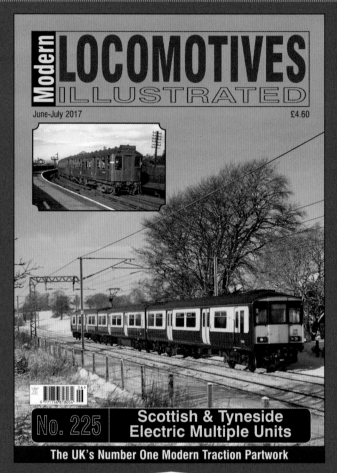

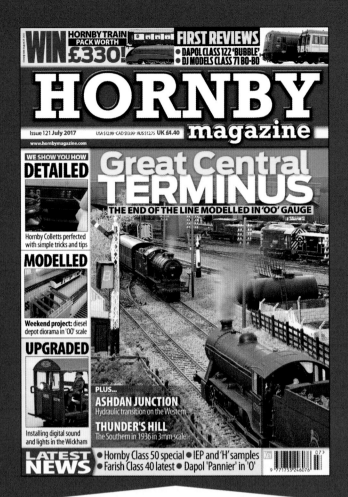
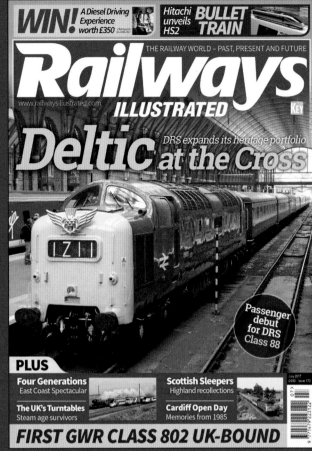

624/17

Modifying the Bulleid Pacifics

Jeremy English, *having made a thorough study of the rebuilding of the Southern Pacific locomotives from 'Spam Can' air-smoothed form, provides full details of this action during 1956/57, and the reasons regarding these modifications.*

In its first year in service, and the Southern Railway's last year, 1949, the down 'Devon Belle' Pullman train is seen at Byfleet & New Haw station hauled by one of the second series of Bulleid 'Merchant Navy' Pacifics, No 21C15 *Rotterdam Lloyd*. In the immediate post-war era the sight of these radical locomotives, complemented by their bright malachite green livery, offset by three yellow stripes, was a ray of sunshine for those austere days. However, to the operating authorities, at a time when maintenance backlogs and rising costs were a daily nightmare, the unconventional features of the locomotives were more of a hindrance than a help. Bulleid had intended the air-smoothed casings to be easily washed in automatic washing machines and the enclosed oil baths to reduce the enginemen's lubrication duties, but the former made it difficult to keep them clean when there were very few washing plants, and the latter made access to the motion for maintenance a nightmare.

In 1938 the Southern Railway was celebrating the success of its Portsmouth main-line electrification schemes. Scheme 1 was via Guildford (which had opened in 1937), and Scheme 2 was via Arundel, which opened on 2 July 1938. After fifteen years of intensive electrification there was little stopping them from completing the long-term plan to electrify most of the system, expected to take another decade or so. Nevertheless, despite funnelling most of the company's capital expenditure to this project, there was recognition that there would still be a need for steam for some years to come. An authority was thus issued to order the construction of ten new express locomotives, the principle requirement being to produce locomotives capable of handling the ever-increasing Continental traffic on the lines to Dover so that they could keep up with electric trains on the Kent main lines which were next in the electrification programme.

Seldom can such a simple order have such unexpected consequences! The Southern Railway's first Chief Mechanical Engineer, Richard Maunsell, had retired at the end of October in the previous year and the principal assistant to the great Nigel Gresley on the

LNER had been appointed to replace him. Oliver Vaughan Snell Bulleid was given full reign to express himself, the first thing to be apparent to observers being his re-liverying of locomotives and rolling stock, starting with the new buffet cars for the Portsmouth Scheme 2 electric units.

The requirement for the new steam locomotives was not, apparently, very urgent, and Bulleid had time to present a number of proposals, his preference being a Mikado (2-8-2) locomotive design as he had had considerable experience with the famous Gresley 'P2' class Mikados, especially *Cock o' The North.* Approval was given to build two prototypes to work the 'Night Ferry' for delivery in 1940 but unfortunately the civil engineers vetoed that project, possibly because they had memories of the Sevenoaks disaster ten years earlier when an express locomotive fitted with a leading pony truck derailed, sadly killing thirteen victims.

In fact, the steam locomotives were not Bulleid's only new design proposals as he had already started the design of a new electric locomotive for similar duties to the steam engines, but both projects were to stall and all plans had to be put on hold as a European war loomed. This changed everything as it became apparent that the Southern Railway would be

on the front line, and thus electrification had to cease, whist every effort had to be made to provide locomotives to support this role.

Bulleid was able to justify the production of the ten new steam locomotives by re-designating them as mixed traffic, rather than express locomotives, and changing the design to a 4-6-2 type. What appeared in 1941, just a short time before the prototype electric machine, was totally different to what had gone before. Perhaps wartime restrictions softened the news, but *Channel Packet,* as the first of the new Pacifics of the 'Merchant Navy' class was named (a nod to the originally-intended duties), was unlike any steam locomotive before it, with what Bulleid termed an 'air-smoothed' casing hiding the traditional circular steam boiler, and a built-up irregularly-shaped smokebox.

The locomotive had many other unconventional features hidden under that casing, notably its inside chain-driven valve gear further encased in an oil bath and activating three cylinders with outside steam admission valves. The wheels also looked odd to British eyes, but were merely an adaption of then-current practise in the U.S.A. The exhaust had no less than five blastpipe nozzles, known as a multiple-jet blastpipe! At a time when what was needed was an ultra-simple

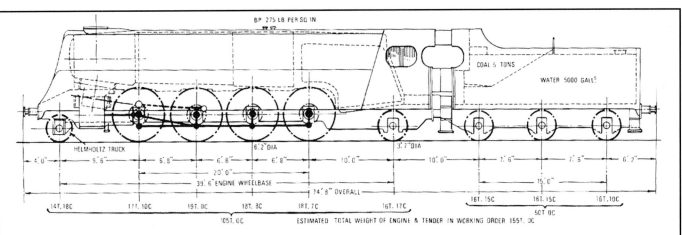

BP 275 LB PER SQ IN

COAL 5 TONS
WATER 5000 GALLS

HELMHOLTZ TRUCK
6' 2" DIA
3' 7" DIA

4' 0" — 9' 6" — 6' 8" — 6' 8" — 6' 8" — 10' 0" — 10' 0" — 7' 6" — 7' 6" — 6' 2"
20' 0"
39' 6" ENGINE WHEELBASE
74' 8" OVERALL
15' 0"

14T. 18C 17T. 10C 19T. 0C 18T. 8C 18T. 7C 16T. 17C 16T. 15C 16T. 15C 16T. 10C
105T. 0C 50T. 0C
ESTIMATED TOTAL WEIGHT OF ENGINE & TENDER IN WORKING ORDER 155T. 0C

Bulleid's final version of his Mikado locomotive of March 1939 for the Eastern Division of the Southern Region showing the Hemholtz truck suspension which was intended to counter the Civil Engineer's objections to the use of a front pony wheel. It looks remarkably like 'Merchant Navy' Pacific *Channel Packet* with a 2-8-2 layout!

locomotive, what Bulleid produced was ultra-complicated. However he had the right intentions; the objective of the self-lubricating valve gear was to minimise the enginemens' time oiling the motion, and the casing was supposed to be easy to wash in automatic washing plants rather than by legions of manual cleaners who were becoming hard to find in wartime.

Modifications came thick and fast during its first few months in service and continued through the war years as the full order of ten machines was delivered. Most notable were a cowl added at the front of the top casing and the fitment of smoke deflectors, both necessary to improve the airflow around the exhaust which had tended to obscure the drivers' vision.

As the war drew to a close and building restrictions were eased, Bulleid carried on with the development of the design. A smaller type of locomotive would be required and, after initially proposing a new form of 2-6-0, he actually scaled down the Pacific design to produce the 'West Country' class which, to uninformed eyes, looked virtually identical to the larger engines! In fact they were, in many respects, the principal alteration being a reduction in length created by shortening the

firebox by twelve inches. Both designs proved to be prodigious steam-raisers, but at the cost of high fuel consumption. The 'Merchant Navy' Pacifics became known as the 'Heavy Pacifics', whilst the 'West Country' class became the 'Light Pacifics'. This distinction was important inasmuch as the former were restricted to a few main lines, whilst the latter could traverse all lines, except the least important branch lines.

Almost as unbelievable to most observers as the production of the first 'Merchant Navy' Pacific was the fact that the Southern Railway went on to order two further batches of ten 4-6-2 locomotives to increase the total to thirty, and to order a total of 110 of the Light Pacifics, nominally creating two classes of the latter, the 'West Country' and the 'Battle of Britain' classes. Construction was virtually continuous from 1945 until 1951, by which time British Railways had been formed and inherited this massive number of Pacific locomotives. As a result of the war the Southern had many totally worn-out engines and was in acute need of new locomotives. The Bulleids were the only new types in production, so that probably accounts for the fact that so many were ordered. Bulleid was in the process of designing a new type of tank engine to replace

the pre-Grouping ones but, being Bulleid, he had complicated the design. That is probably all we need to say about the 'Leaders' here!

Ironically, this massive construction programme seems at odds with a Southern Railway plan issued in 1946 which foresaw the elimination of steam by 1955, and the construction of large numbers of electric and diesel locomotives, the latter to take over from steam where electrification might take years to justify or, in the case of branch lines and the far-flung parts of the Southern empire in the West Country, never take place. An order was placed to build two (subsequently three) main-line diesels to be built by English Electric. These didn't appear until after British Railways had taken over and the Southern Railway's plans had been modified.

Modifications to the Southern Pacifics had continued during the production runs, but British Railways was soon somewhat alarmed to find that the engines remained unreliable when compared to other modern designs that it had inherited. Nevertheless, when making a comparison with the latter in the famous 'Great Locomotive Exchanges' of 1948, the Bulleid engines had proven to have what were possibly the finest boilers of all, but the rest of the design did not score so well.

The appearance of the air-smoothed Bulleid Pacific locomotives gave rise to 'Marmite' opinions amongst observers — you either loved the look or loathed it. The 'Merchant Navy' Pacific No 35024 – BR gave them conventional numbers – was one of the final ten engines of the class built after nationalisation and displays its final form at Eastleigh on 13 March 1956, just a month after the first rebuild, No 35018, had appeared. No 35024 *East Asiatic Company*, pictured here at Eastleigh depot, would not disappear into the Works for modification for another three years, having had a full general overhaul two years before this photograph was taken. On this visit it had just had a light classified overhaul at which it received plain coupling rods and an unspecified modification, and had been returned to traffic on the first of the month. Platform 14 Collection MF1745

Seen under the hoist alongside Plymouth (Friary) locomotive shed is a slightly schizophrenic *Dartmoor* in October 1949, bearing both its Bulleid number 21C121 with an added 'S' for 'Southern', and its new BR smokebox numberplate proclaiming it to be No 34021. It was just 21 months old at this time, and more of these locomotives were appearing every week from Brighton Works. Observers questioned why the Southern was building so many of these complicated and powerful locomotives in a time of austerity, the so-called Light Pacifics being only marginally less powerful and lighter than their earlier brethren of the 'Merchant Navy' class. If familiarity breeds contempt, there were many who felt the latter emotion as some of them were used on the sparsely-trafficked lines in the West Country, somewhat amusingly known as the 'Withered Arm' lines, often on trains of just two coaches.

British Railways was so concerned about the failings of the Bulleid Pacifics that construction of the very last machine ordered, No 34110, was delayed, whilst consideration was given to modifying the design to incorporate conventional valve gear and a reduction to two cylinders. This proved to be one step too far for the cash-strapped nationalised concern, so the engine was completed to match its class-mates. A survey also showed that the utilisation of the Southern Pacifics was far below that of comparative designs. Brighton, for example, where the engines had been built in the Works opposite the running sheds, had four Light Pacifics for three diagrams, but often had none available for work, and Salisbury

had seven engines for just two diagrams in 1953! Thus in the early 1950s the Southern Region was still suffering from an acute locomotive shortage yet, at times, ten per cent of the Pacific fleet was in store, so something had to be done.

Just as the locomotives started to gain an almost uniform appearance following standardisation of the smoke deflector length (but still with some exceptions, Nos 34004-06 and 35020 having very long ones), and a new-style of cab, a programme which took until 9 March 1957 to complete, the first evidence of action to address some of their failings came in 1952. Three of each type (Nos 35012/13/21 and 34011/43/65) had the tender 'raves' removed and received a number

of modifications 'in an endeavour to eliminate as many as possible of the troublesome features of the locomotives short of a major modification', to quote the report on the proposed modifications to the 'Merchant Navy' and 'West Country' classes of locomotives from Brighton Works in January 1955. This was the report drawn up under Ronald Jarvis that led to the massive programme which transformed the locomotives out of all recognition.

It is noted that the report described 'modifications', the term 'rebuilt' associated with the engines coming later but, as it is the common term used for the locomotives, they will be henceforth be known as 'rebuilt' herein.

As they got older, the 'Spam Cans', as they were often called in recollection of the unpleasant wartime canned meat product, accumulated oil spillages under the air-smoothed casings. During the 1950s and 1960a there were increasing numbers of fires caused by the oil igniting, and this became another bone of contention and another reason to 'defrock' them. Curiously, No 34057, the 'Battle of Britain' class Pacific named in recognition of the famous Biggin Hill airfield, would never lose its casing, it being simply repaired after the incident involving an oil bath fire on the engine on 22 May 1961 when it was between Hamble and Netley while working a Brighton to Bournemouth train. It would miss the rebuilding programme that involved sixty of the 110 Light Pacifics by having a general overhaul three months before the programme started on them, and not having another until five months after the last locomotive was rebuilt. *K.W. Wightman*

The first Bulleid Pacific to be rebuilt was No 35018 *British India Line*, which emerged in its sparkling new form from Eastleigh Works on 7 February 1956. It had a history of uniqueness in its original condition, having been built with fabricated rather than cast driving wheels, and having run with the equally-unique coal-weighing tender No 3343 for three months in 1952. It then acquired the 6,000gallon tender, No 3346 (built for No 35024), which was cut-down while the locomotive was rebuilt. It remained unique in its rebuilt form, with the bend in the ejector pipe above the nameplate rather than just to the rear of the smokebox as on all the other 'Merchant Navy' Pacifics (the Light Pacifics had straight ones) and, initially at least, no smoke deflector handrails. Here it is seen having just been inspected at Waterloo in its new form in February 1956.
S. Townroe/Colour-Rail 312040ST

There were a few other experiments or modifications before the rebuilding commenced described in the report, in addition to the tender alterations (tenders are even more complex, and thus interesting, than the locomotives!). Two 'Merchant Navy' class Pacifics, Nos 35022 and 35019, received single blastpipes and chimneys for a while, the former whilst undergoing tests at the Rugby testing station and the latter until rebuilding. Evidently this was not a success. A programme was initiated in 1953 to re-position the safety valves behind the dome, rather than in front of it, and following the derailment of No 35020 at Crewkerne in 1953, because of a broken crank axle, new crank axles were supplied which, rather significantly, made provision for one of the major modifications to be made under the rebuilding programme. The report stated 'An eccentric will be placed on the crank axle in place of the existing chain-driving sprocket'. Provision was made for this latter modification when the crank axle was redesigned

The report had two interesting dates in it. The annual savings to be gained were shown in a table covering a period ending in 1975, and the net estimated ultimate saving of £2,051,402 assumed that the date of scrapping would be 1987. This showed how Southern Region thinking under British Railways had changed totally from that of the Southern Railway just ten years earlier.

Rebuilding was expected to start in 1955, with six locomotives released to traffic that year, and nine in the following year (Order HO 7998), but delays meant that it wasn't until 9 February 1956 that No 35018 was unveiled to the world and the programme slipped for one full year. It looked like a completely new and utterly different machine, with echoes of BR Standard classes in its overall appearance. Since the details of this are now so well-known it is unnecessary to list all these, but it may be relevant to stress how little had changed.

The report's suggestions were a model of competence and economy, utilising as much of the original locomotives as possible whilst doing away with the unreliable features. Despite the fact that the shape of the boiler could now be seen since the air smoothed plating had gone, it was still the same prodigious steam-raiser it had always been. A circular smokebox replaced the odd construction that Bulleid had designed, but the multiple blastpipe remained. Most obvious was the new outside valve gear, but it was still of the same Walschaerts design, albeit with traditional rods rather than chains. The oil bath had gone, and the inside cylinder was replaced by a new design. Together with the new valve gear, this latter was possibly the single most significant item in the rebuilding, whilst the outside cylinders were re-used. The cab was little changed, the smokebox door remained with its characteristic oval shape,

The 'Merchant Navy' Pacific No 35018 *British India Line* spent its first few months in general service as the 'Bournemouth Belle' locomotive, it being allocated to Nine Elms shed which handled this prestigious train. Although by 5 May 1956, when this photograph was taken at Vauxhall, it had acquired smoke deflector handrails, its right-hand side also displayed unique features, having an oddly-shaped front sanding filler (as it did on the other side as well), together with 'kinks' in the clack-valve feed pipes; the latter would be altered later. This engine would return to the main line in 2017, making its first test run on 18 May, some 61 years after this photograph was taken! D. Preston/Colour-Rail 97451

The first two rebuilds, 'Merchant Navy' Pacifics Nos 35018, seen here on the 'Bournemouth Belle', and 35020, in the bay, are pictured alongside each other at the western end of Southampton (Central) station in May 1956. No 35020 *Bibby Line* was effectively the first production rebuild, displaying the different pipe runs and filler pipes that would be common to all the remaining engines. It was used to test the modifications during a series of trials in May and June 1956 and was the only engine of the class to work with an unmodified tender, No 3345, which was attached so that cables between the locomotive and the Western Region dynamometer car could be more easily secured than on a cut-down tender. No 35020 had been the only engine of its class to be fitted with extra-long smoke deflectors in its original state and was the stand-by locomotive (but never used) for the 1948 Locomotive Exchange trials. It was notorious for breaking its crank axle at Crewkerne in 1953, an incident that led to all the Bulleid Pacifics being temporarily stopped for inspection, and the loan of various 'V2' class 2-6-2s, 'B1' and 'Black Five' 4-6-0s, and BR Standard classes to the Southern Region for a few weeks during that year.
B.J. Swain/Colour-Rail BRS375

the brake-gear remained, and the frames were re-used.

Perhaps the most revealing feature of the whole rebuilding programme was that it only took around two to three weeks to rebuild a locomotive. This was because they were rebuilt at the same time they were due a general overhaul, which also explains the order in which they were called in for rebuilding, something that otherwise appears to be random. For example, the first general overhaul for the 51st engine done, No 35024, undertaken from 5 April to 15 April 1954, took six weeks, whilst its rebuilding and general overhaul from 26 February to 25 April 1959 amounted to nine weeks. The prototype Light Pacific, No 34001, was rebuilt, and had a general overhaul from 21 October to 23 November 1957 – a mere five weeks! Its previous general overhaul had taken nine weeks, but that included Christmas (29 November 1954 to 22 January 1955).

The 'Merchant Navy' class Pacifics were rebuilt in two tranches of fifteen, split into five before and ten after the summer seasons – none were out of service in August or September, until the final batch was done in 1959. The Light Pacifics were split into four batches of fifteen, but that went on all year round. The modification completion dates and order numbers are shown in Table One.

Whilst no 'Merchant Navy' Pacifics received general overhauls without being rebuilt after No 35018 emerged, there were some 'escapees' among the Light Pacifics. There were also no significant alterations to the rebuilds, with one small exception. After No 35001 in August 1959, small 'pockets' were found in the lower edge of the smoke deflectors to allow extended valve spindles to be withdrawn for servicing (Nos 35019 and 35024 simply had holes cut that allowed ash and soot to get on to the spindles). Earlier engines then received this modification in due course.

The Light Pacific rebuild programme started at the same time as the first phase of the Kent Coast Electrification Scheme commenced, and the first 15 rebuilds (HO 8428) were sent to Eastern Section sheds, which enabled the two BR 'Britannia' Pacifics, Nos 70004 and 70014, to be transferred to the London Midland Region in 1958.

There were two bays for rebuilding until 1958 when three and in 1960 when four engines were worked on simultaneously, so if three engines became due general overhauls at around the same time one would 'escape' rebuilding, and this explains why all three of the 1952 Light Pacific 'tender rebuilds' were not done, as Nos 34011 and 34043 became due, whilst No 34005, the first Light Pacific rebuild, was still being completed, and before any

others were done. When the third Light Pacific, No 34065, became due, Nos 34003 and 34013 occupied the rebuilding bays. The three 'tender rebuilds' were the first locomotives not rebuilt to receive the first, left and right-facing later BR crests, and pioneered the final lining and painting schemes for the remaining 'Spam Cans'. When cut-down in 1952, they had a rather clumsy layout with the cabside lining taken to its lower edge, rather than having a black panel at the bottom. Other than these three locomotives, with the exception of No 34080 in November 1957, all Light Pacifics due a general overhaul were rebuilt until the first batch of fifteen was completed.

Perhaps some of the other modifications to the three 1952 engines made them a little special as, other than their 'escapes' noted earlier, none of them ever had another general overhaul, although they became amongst the earliest engines to be withdrawn, No 34043 being the first, together with No 34035, on 8 June 1963, No 34011 on 30 November 1963 (the 8th), and No 34065 in April 1964. It has been reported that No 34043 was one of the 'black sheep of the family'.

It is curious that no more tenders were cut down between 1952 and the start of the rebuilding programme in 1956, but thereafter all tenders attached to rebuilt engines were cut down. It may seem that there was a long gap before tenders attached to locomotives not being rebuilt were cut down, but this was because there was a lot of tender exchanging going on so that rebuilt engines received the larger 5,500gallon tenders that were originally built with the final forty of these engines (Nos 34071-110), and these were cut down whilst the engines were rebuilt. Most of these final forty had had their first general overhauls during 1955/56, and thus were not due more until 1959/60, so they did not feature in the first batches of thirty Light Pacific rebuilds of 1957/58. The 1958/59 slots were then used for the first five of the second batch of fifteen 'Merchant Navy' Pacifics — five in 1958 and ten in 1959 (HO 9199).

Table One
Modification dates and order numbers of Bulleid Pacifics

5	'Merchant Navy' Pacifics	14/2/56 to 7/7/56	HO 7998
10	'Merchant Navy' Pacifics	12/12/56 to 30/3/57	HO 7998
15	Light Pacifics	29/6/57 to 7/4/58	HO 8428
5	'Merchant Navy' Pacifics	23/4/58 to 5/7/58	HO 9199
15	Light Pacifics	9/8/58 to 29/3/59	HO 9361
10	'Merchant Navy' Pacifics	25/4/59 to 24/10/59	HO 9199
15	Light Pacifics	23/6/60 to 8/10/60	HO 9886
15	Light Pacifics	22/10/60 to 13/5/61	HO 9903

HO – Heavy overhaul

No 35016 *Rotterdam Lloyd* was the only engine of the 'Merchant Navy' class to work on the Eastern Division following rebuilding. It had been allocated to Stewarts Lane shed from June 1956, and returned there after it was called into Eastleigh for its general overhaul two years later, its rebuilding taking place from 1 May to 14 June 1958. It was a regular engine on the 'Golden Arrow' as the two BR 'Britannia' Pacifics were returned to the Eastern Region earlier that year. It was transferred to Nine Elms shed during the period ending 14 June 1959 so it is a little strange that this photograph of the locomotive heading the up 'Golden Arrow' at South Willesborough on the approach to Ashford is dated 6 July 1959. Platform 14 Collection MF1744

The first of the Light Pacifics to be rebuilt was No 34005 *Barnstaple* (but see the text for doubts!). In these three photographs by Stephen Townroe it is seen at various stages of the work. New frames were needed as the original ones were badly fractured as was the middle cylinder. The latter didn't matter, as a new inside cylinder casting, which incorporated the saddle for the new cylindrical smokebox, was the major part of the modification and is prominent in the first of this sequence of illustrations. The new frames do not look new, as they were actually seven years old, having been cut at Ashford in 1950 as one of two sets of spares for the class, possibly the only major component of any of the Bulleid Pacifics to have any connection with the Eastern Division. Bradley records that frame fracturing was a common failing on the Pacifics, and that these were usually repaired by welding. He states that 39 out of 43 Pacifics inspected at Eastleigh Works from 1960 to 1964 had deep fractures ahead of the leading coupled wheels, the rebuilt engines having the worse problems. S. Townroe/Colour-Rail 308887ST

The boiler and firebox were unchanged, merely overhauled, and 'West Country' Pacific No 34005 *Barnstaple* received No 1284, which had seen service on Light Pacifics Nos 21C126 and 34057, having come off the latter at its previously-mentioned general overhaul that was completed on 5 January 1957. No 34005 *Barnstaple* kept it until its withdrawal in October 1966, thus very little of what we see in these photographs had been part of the engine that came in for rebuilding except, maybe, the front buffer beam! Perhaps the wheels were original; certainly most of the pipework and motion were new as were the nameplates themselves, even though they would now need new mounting frames on the new running plates. The tender was No 3358, a 5,500gallon one from No 34094 *Mortehoe*, the first 26 rebuilds acquiring larger tenders from the 34071-34110 series which had 5,500gallon 9ft wide tenders, rebuilds from earlier locomotives having their cabs widened to 9ft from the original 8ft 6in. S. Townroe/Colour-Rail 308889

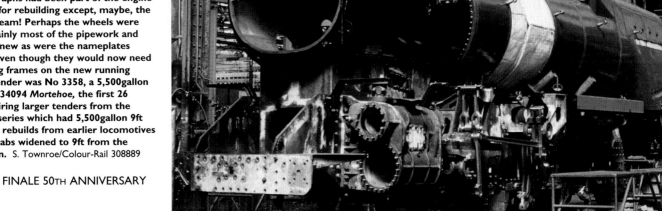

'Grandad's Hammer' might have been a better name for the machine which is seen nearing completion in June 1956. The enormous length of the new smokebox is very evident here; usually this is disguised by the smoke deflectors. The amount of 'gubbins' on the running plate and on the boiler itself shows how much easier normal maintenance would be on the modified engines. There would only be one real alteration to the rebuilt machines, which would be the provision of small pockets in the slope of the running plate, and in the edge of the deflectors to access the tail rods of the piston valve spindles, longer ones being provided later in the modification programme. The original short ones are clearly visible here, and access for their maintenance would need the bottom part of the deflectors and the slope of the running plate to be removed until the pockets were provided from mid-1959.
S. Townroe/Colour-Rail 308888

All of the first tranche of fifteen Light Pacific rebuilds completed in 1957 were sent to the Eastern Division of the Southern Region, the Pacific pictured here being the second rebuild, No 34027 *Taw Valley*, seen under the famous white cliffs between Dover and Folkestone near Shakespeare cliff tunnels in 1958. This engine, perhaps unsurprisingly, would be one of the earliest rebuilds to be withdrawn, in August 1964, when it became due for its first general overhaul after rebuilding, the last engine to be rebuilt being No 34104 in May 1961. Only seven out of sixty rebuilds ever had general overhauls as rebuilds, although 23 of the remaining fifty originals had them thereafter until all general overhauls ceased in February 1964.   G. Parry Collection/Colour-Rail 314950

The twelfth Light Pacific rebuild, No 34026 *Yes Taw*, is pictured at Ashford on 10 May 1958 with the 9.08am Charing Cross to Sandwich service in a view that illustrates the locomotive's wider 9ft 5,500gallon tender, No 3364. This tender was purloined from No 34104 *Bere Alston* that had come in for a light intermediate overhaul in January of that year while No 34026 was being rebuilt. No 34104 would be rebuilt in May 1961, keeping the 8ft 6in tender that it had been given from No 34026. D. Ovenden/Colour-Rail 18047

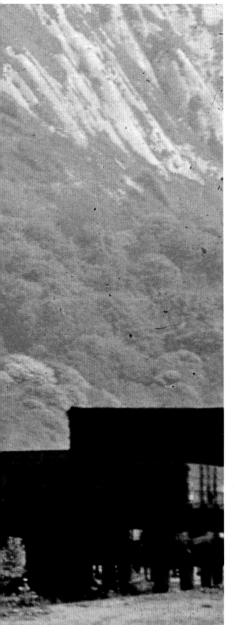

According to Bradley, the first Light Pacific to be rebuilt was to have been No 34040, which entered Eastleigh on 24 April 1957 for a light intermediate overhaul, which makes it seem an odd choice, and it was being prepared for reconstruction when No 34005 failed with fractured frames and a damaged inside cylinder. No 34040 merely had a normal general overhaul and returned to work unmodified (but see below: Bradley may have meant No 34045). Thus No 34005 became the first rebuild (or perhaps it didn't!) The frames were so badly damaged that the locomotive which emerged as the rebuilt No 34005 had brand-new frames and, as it is generally considered that a locomotive is identified by its frames, surely this was a brand-new engine utilising parts from the scrapped No 34005, so should have born the number 34111, and should not have been regarded as a rebuild either!

Leaving that identity question aside, there were a few interesting oddities and escapees during the period 1957-59. No 34045 seems to have been a more likely candidate for the first rebuild as it arrived at Eastleigh for a general overhaul just a week before No 34005. It returned to service unreconstructed, but with another type of modification which entailed the fitment of a new form of spark arrestor. This engine thus became one of only two to display the first version of the later BR crest (left and right facing lions) on a tender, with raves still in place; the other was, as mentioned earlier, No 34080 which was the only engine to have a general overhaul without being rebuilt, nor having its tender

cut down during the timespan of the first batch of fifteen rebuilds. All Light Pacific rebuilds sported the new crests.

The spark arrestor made the steaming of No 34045 far worse, so it returned to Eastleigh to have it removed in July 1958, but something must have gone seriously awry as No 34018 came in a week later and was rebuilt, but emerged four weeks before No 34045. The latter's work was upgraded to a general overhaul from a light overhaul (it had only run 54,863miles since its 1957 general overhaul) and the locomotive emerged rebuilt after eleven weeks in Eastleigh Works.

Another unexpected arrival at Eastleigh Works was No 34066 on 17 February 1958 following the Lewisham disaster. It wasn't due a general overhaul so it was quickly repaired, but its tender had been badly crushed, and this was rebuilt without raves, the engine becoming the first 'Spam Can' (the original design gave birth to a number of nicknames) after the three 1952 ones to get a cut-down tender. Thereafter, all locomotives undergoing general overhauls until No 34078 had their tenders cut down, whether or not the locomotives were rebuilt.

Two more Light Pacifics came in for general overhauls in April but were not rebuilt as the next batch of five 'Merchant Navy' Pacifics were being dealt with (HO 9199). These were Nos 34067 and 34070, both of whose tenders were cut-down, and are both still at work today! The second batch of Light Pacifics (HO 9361) divided the last 'Merchant Navy' order (HO 9199).

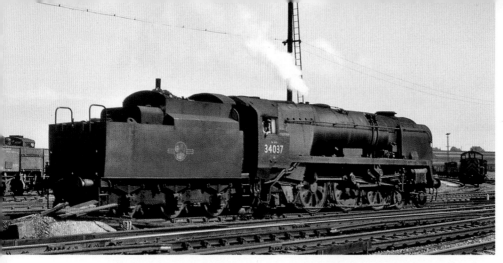

The 'West Country' class Light Pacific No 34037 *Clovelly,* pictured here at Eastleigh on 29 June 1967, was rebuilt in March 1958 and, like 34104 *Bere Alston,* retained its somewhat mismatched 8ft 6in wide tender as almost all the 9ft wide ones had been transferred to earlier rebuilds. This Light Pacific's nameplate backing strip has been repainted red, with the name picked out in gold paint. Curiously, Nos 34078/91/99/102/107 all retained their 9ft tenders even though they were never rebuilt, thus 35 rebuilds had 9ft tenders and 25 had 8ft 6in ones, although three of the latter were to be fitted with new tanks, as seen in the next photograph. Bill Wright/Platform 14 BW006

In preparation for the third tranche (HO 9886) of Light Pacifics, the third rebuilding bay was started, and No 34028 joined the last 'Merchant Navy' Pacifics in the Works. Nos 34110 and 34063 came in for general overhauls and emerged unaltered, but thereafter only Nos 34073, 34083 and 34075 were overlooked. The latter was then fitted with the spark arrester which had come off No 34045 and it doesn't seem to have been problematic on that engine. Since those engines (Nos 34073/75/80/83/110) from the final forty built that did come in for general overhauls during the first rebuilding programme of thirty engines were all returned to work unmodified (except their tenders, other than on No 34080), this may be an indication that preference was given to older engines where there was a possible conflict.

Nos 34062/79/41/81/76 and 34078/72/74/54 came in for general overhauls in that order, whilst the last ten 'Merchant Navy' Pacifics were being dealt with, and thus escaped modification. For some reason the tenders of Nos 34078/72/74/54 were not cut down, but the next entry, No 34049 in October 1959, was given special treatment and a cut-down tender. This was the 'interregnum' before the last batches of rebuilds (HO 9886/9903) were authorised, so Eastleigh Works decided to try and improve

the smoke-deflecting capacity of the remaining 'Spam Cans' and made some hideous alterations to the engine's front end; the engine returned to normal in February 1960. A week after No 34049 went into the Works, No 34035, the next in, received yet another variation of the strange front end. No record seems to have been kept as to when this was removed and, as noted earlier, it was the first Pacific withdrawn (along with No 34011) on 8 June 1963.

Eastleigh Works probably lost interest in these modified originals once authority was given for the rebuilding of a further thirty engines (HO 9886/9903), but when these became the last such orders it took the cudgel up once again, ten months after the last rebuild emerged in March 1962 when No 34064 came in for a general overhaul. On 28 April 1962 this engine emerged with a Giesl Ejector, replacing the multiple-jet blastpipe. It was to prove to be the last modification, and was spectacularly successful. It was intended to reduce instances of fire-throwing, but actually made the engine livelier as well, No 34064 being considered to be the equal of the larger 'Merchant Navy' Pacifics on the road.

Everything then changed, as just 47 weeks later withdrawals started, the first ones to go being engines transferred to the Western Region at the end of 1962 when that region took over responsibility for Southern Region lines west of Wilton. They did not want them (they were all originals anyway), and they sent them back to the Southern who no longer had any use for them, so withdrawals were inevitable.

The year 1963 was a bad year for steam as Dr Beeching pronounced and BR accelerated its abolition of steam. In 1964 the Southern Region got permission to electrify the line to Bournemouth, with diesels to Weymouth, and the days of the Southern Pacific locomotives were numbered, ending, in BR terms, on 9 July 1967. So perhaps the final 'modifications' were done by the scrap merchant, but there is a postscript. From a total of 140 engines 109¼ were scrapped, the other 30¾ Southern Pacifics remain to this day, most restored to working order, so the Bulleids live on! The '¾' is No 35029 as a sectioned exhibit at the National Railway Museum at York, perhaps the final 'modification', unless No 35011 becomes the first unrebuilt Bulleid Pacific!

The story of Light Pacific tenders is quite complicated. In addition to the two types being swapped around, seemingly at random, four of them had to have new tanks between 1958 and 1960 because the tanks were notoriously difficult to keep watertight. The first was 5,500gallon 9ft wide tender No 3354 in December 1958, and it was followed by three of the 4,500gallon 8ft 6in tenders, the first being No 3313 in January 1959 that was attached to No 34039 *Boscastle,* as seen here. The old tank on tender No 3354 was re-used on a 4,500gallon underframe, No 3271, attached to 'Battle of Britain' class Pacific No 34062. All the new tanks were 9ft wide and carried 5,250 gallons of water. They were distinguished by the fact they did not have a visible fire-iron tunnel like the original tenders alongside the coal bunker and a higher top for the rear deck. Similar 5,250gallon tanks were provided for 'Merchant Navy' tenders, including the former coal-weighing tender, the latter in 1962. C. Boocock

Clapham Junction in the 1960s

Lunchtime at Clapham Junction cutting, to the west of the station, on Saturday, 1 June 1963, sees rebuilt 'Merchant Navy' class Pacific No 35015 *Rotterdam Lloyd* in charge of the down 'Bournemouth Belle' about to pass classmate No 35028 *Clan Line* at the head of the 10.08am Bournemouth to Waterloo train. Viewed from the road bridge at Battersea Rise, the rails curving away to the right are those of the Brighton line. Brian Stephenson

By the 1960s the writing was on the wall for Southern Region steam, but Clapham Junction was, as this photographic feature shows, still full of interest as **Andrew Wilson** *relates.*

Clapham Junction station sprawled at the bottom of St. John's Hill and Lavender Hill and was carried over the Falcon Road on substantial girders, but was not in Clapham but Battersea, which itself was part of the borough of Wandsworth. The working-class name of Battersea Junction did not have the more fashionable appeal of the title adopted, Clapham Junction, which in itself was a geographical nonsense. Dominating the area was the departmental store of Arding & Hobbs, along with the plethora of newsagents, tobacconists, school outfitters, and shops that we took for granted, but have long-since disappeared, thanks to the omnipresent supermarkets. Over the years, London Transport buses, trams, and

trolleybuses served the station, but the nearest underground station was Clapham Common.

The sprawling expanse of the station, a small matter of seventeen platforms in 1960, justifiably claimed to be the busiest station in the country and was synonymous with crowds of people, endless steps, sooty grime-encrusted windows, faded paintwork, wooden-floored footbridges, and a forbidding subway. Electric-multiple-units came and went with that particular aroma associated with the 750volt dc system used, yet it was the steam-hauled trains that endowed Clapham Junction with that aura of magic that drew the enthusiast back time after time.

Clapham Junction opened on 2 March 1863 as a joint station by the London & South Western, London, Brighton & South Coast, and the West London Extension railways as an interchange station for their lines. There were no

less than six junctions that served the station – Falcon Junction at the south end of the station where the West London line joins the Brighton slow lines, Ludgate Junction at the eastern end of the Windsor line platforms to the West London line, Latchmere South West Junction connecting the West London line to the Windsor lines at Ludgate Junction, Latchmere Main Junction connecting the West London line to the Brighton line at Falcon Junction and the West London Extension Junction and junction for Waterloo and Pouparts Junction where the low-level and high-level approaches to Victoria station divide.

The station's days of steam ended on 9 July 1967 after 104 years. The occasional steam special still passes through the junction, but the modern railway is now a very different place to that of the 1960s yet, at heart, Clapham Junction is still the same busy station.

No less than 23 BR Standard '3MT' 2-6-2Ts found their way to Nine Elms shed for use on the empty stock movements in and around Clapham Junction, station pilot duties at Waterloo, and on the 'Kenney Belle'. On 16 July 1964 a work-stained No 82017 arrives at Clapham Junction with the 'Bournemouth Belle' Pullman cars that will be cleaned and serviced before returning to Bournemouth on the down working. Brian Stephenson

The BR Standard '4MT' 2-6-4Ts were a common sight at Clapham Junction, but rarely were they seen in such spotless condition as this. Nos 80143 and 80137, both allocated to Nine Elms shed at the time, were given what amounted to an exhibition finish to top and tail the empty stock of the funeral train for Sir Winston Churchill from Clapham Junction sidings into London (Waterloo) on Saturday, 30 January 1965. Brian Stephenson

One of the curiosities of Clapham Junction was the unadvertised rush-hour service to and from Kensington Olympia for Post Office workers. During LB&SCR and Southern Railway days the service was worked by 0-4-2Ts and 0-4-4Ts, and in British Railways days this was a Stewarts Lane working. On 22 August 1962 an 'H' class 0-4-4T, No 31542, has just arrived at Clapham Junction's Platform 17 with the 5.35pm service from Kensington Olympia. This service remained steam-operated until July 1967, with BR Standard 2-6-4Ts, 2-6-2Ts, and Ivatt '2MT' 2-6-2Ts the chosen motive power.
Brian Stephenson

To the west of Battersea Rise the former L&SWR four-track main line to Wimbledon and Woking and the south-west assumes a slightly more rural aspect as it runs out of Clapham cutting. On Sunday, 28 March 1965, rebuilt Weymouth-allocated 'Merchant Navy' class Pacific No 35007 *Aberdeen Commonwealth* heads south-west when in charge of the down 'Bournemouth Belle', the Western Division's premier steam working. Brian Stephenson

On 10 June 1962 Stewarts Lane-based BR Standard '4MT' 4-6-0 No 75069 hurries through Clapham Junction when in charge of the 4.38pm London (Victoria) to Brighton via Oxted train. One of fifteen BR-built Standard '4MT' 4-6-0s allocated to the Southern Region and fitted with double chimneys and blastpipes, Nos 75065-79 were highly-regarded and often used on '5MT' duties. Brian Stephenson

Many of the inter-regional holiday trains from the Brighton and Worthing areas destined for the Midlands and further north were routed through Clapham Junction on to the West London Extension line through to the London Midland Region via Kensington Olympia and Mitre Junction to Willesden Junction. On Saturday, 18 August 1962 Brighton-allocated rebuilt 'Battle of Britain' class Pacific No 34089 *602 Squadron* takes the line from Clapham South Junction to Latchmere Junction *en route* to the London Midland Region. Brian Stephenson

Right: **Between February 1959 and August 1963 Nine Elms depot was allocated fifteen different former GWR '5700'/'8750' class 0-6-0PTs for use on the empty coaching-stock movements into and out of Waterloo. No 9770 was at Nine Elms from February 1959 until July 1963 and is seen with a train of serviced carriages *en route* to Waterloo.** Brian Stephenson

On Saturday, 30 June 1962, Brighton shed's 'Battle of Britain' class Pacific No 34057 *Biggin Hill* passes through Clapham Junction at the head of the 1.55pm Brighton to London (Victoria) via Oxted working. To the local train-spotters the appearance of an unmodified Bulleid Pacific would result in shouts of 'Spam Cam' or 'Flat Top' — perhaps derogatory, but descriptive. No 34057 would remain in service until May 1967 when withdrawn from Salisbury shed with a cracked middle cylinder. Brian Stephenson

Stewarts Lane's BR Standard '4MT' 2-6-4T No 80034 has just pulled away from Clapham Junction off the West London Extension line with a military special formed of Eastern Region stock with what appears to be a mix of Gresley and Thompson designs bound for the Oxted and Lewes line on 27 April 1963. No 80034 will almost certainly have come on at Kensington Olympia having taken over the train from an Eastern Region locomotive. Brian Stephenson

The West London Extension line ensured that Western, Midland, and Eastern region locomotives were regularly seen passing through Clapham Junction on inter-regional workings, although outside-cylinder former GWR classes were banned because of clearance issues with their cylinders. On 24 August 1962 Willesden-allocated Stanier '8F' 2-8-0 No 48603, coupled to a Fowler tender, pulls away from Clapham Junction with a Willesden Junction to Norwood yard transfer freight. Brian Stephenson

On 6 June 1962 former L&SWR Drummond 'M7' class 0-4-4T No 30378 arrives at Clapham Junction with the empty coaching stock off 'The Statesman' ocean liner express from Southampton. 'The Statesman' was run in conjunction with the sailings of the American liner *United States* that at the time held the Blue Ribbon for the fastest Atlantic crossing. No 30378 appears to have been borrowed by Nine Elms shed as it was officially a Bournemouth locomotive at the time, but interestingly does not carry Bournemouth's 71B shedplate. Brian Stephenson

Bottom: **BR Standard '5MT' 4-6-0 No 73089,** running without its *Maid of Astolat* nameplates and allocated to Guildford shed, wheels the 18.09 Waterloo to Basingstoke train through Clapham Junction on 16 August 1966. The nameplate has only recently been removed as its location can be clearly seen on the footplate valance. No 73089 took the name *Maid of Astolat* from withdrawn Urie 'N15' class 4-6-0 No 30744. Brian Stephenson

Bottom right: **Maunsell 3-cylinder 'W' class 2-6-4T No 31920** leaves the West London Extension line platform at Clapham Junction at the head of a Willesden Junction to Norwood yard transfer freight on 7 November 1962. Designed to work the heavy cross-London inter-regional freights, the 'W' class tanks were occasionally used on the empty coaching stock movements into and out of Waterloo station, but were banned from working passenger trains after 'River' class 2-6-4T No A800 *River Cray* derailed at speed while approaching Sevenoaks when in charge of the 5.00pm London (Cannon Street) to Deal Pullman car express on 24 August 1927. Brian Stephenson

The Urie and Maunsell principal freight design for the L&SWR and Southern Railway was the 'S15' class 4-6-0. On 18 June 1962 one of the earlier Urie types, No 30507, passes Clapham Junction in charge of a lengthy Nine Elms yard to Southampton fitted freight. Behind No 30507 is the Clapham Junction 'A' signal box that partially collapsed on 10 May 1965, effectively closing the station.
Brian Stephenson

Although the Southern Region had its own allocation of BR Standard '4MT' 2-6-0s, No 76044 was not one of them as it was allocated to Woodford Halse shed when this photograph was taken on 15 May 1964. Passing from Clapham Junction station into the cutting, the BR-built Mogul is in charge of the 15.54 Waterloo to Basingstoke train. It would appear that this locomotive was being worked down to Eastleigh Works for repair. The lines seen to the right are the Central Division ones to Brighton. Brian Stephenson

Top right: **At the beginning of the 1960s the empty carriage stock workings into and out of Waterloo were worked by an eclectic mix of locomotives, ranging from BR Standard tank engines to 'H16' Pacific tanks, to 'King Arthur' and 'Lord Nelson' 4-6-0s. On 24 May 1962 Nine Elms-based former LB&SCR 'E4' class 0-6-2T No 32557 is seen here at Clapham Junction carriage sidings making up a train for a down Waterloo service.** Brian Stephenson

Bescot-allocated Stanier 'Black Five' 4-6-0 No 44873 brings a cross-London freight train from Willesden Junction and the West London Extension line slowly into Platform 17 at Clapham Junction on 13 October 1962. The check-rail on the adjacent line indicates how tight the curve from the station to Latchmere Junction was, and both passenger and freight workings observed the strict speed limits imposed. Brian Stephenson

Brighton shed's Maunsell-designed 'V' or 'Schools' class 4-4-0 No 30901 *Winchester* is working hard as it passes Clapham Junction in charge of the tightly-timed 4.38pm London (Victoria) to Brighton via Oxted train on the overcast afternoon of 11 March 1962. One of the locomotives of the class fitted with a Lemaître exhaust by Bulleid in August 1942, this 'Schools' class engine is in its final year of service, and would be withdrawn in December 1962. Brian Stephenson

Southampton boat trains

*Although boat trains to and from Southampton docks had been running since L&SWR days, in this brief feature, **Rex Kennedy,** working from extensive research by the late Michael Harris, mainly concentrates on the steam era in British Railways days of these interesting trains that many of us still remember.*

The most noteworthy post-war event in the history of the docks at Southampton was the 1950 opening of the Ocean Liner Terminal on the Ocean Dock (originally known as the White Star Dock) which was the principal dock for the transatlantic ocean liners, including, of course, the short-lived but immortal *RMS Titanic* in April 1912. The new terminal building, by far the longest such structure within the docks, was probably a forerunner of modern airport termini as it incorporated such niceties as covered platforms for trains on both sides. From the eastern one we see SR 'Battle of Britain' Pacific No 34081 *92 Squadron* departing for London in 1959. Escalators were also provided to the departure lounges on the upper floor, direct covered telescopic gangways to the loading doors on the ships, and luggage conveyors. Sadly, its useful life was very short, it being demolished in 1983, although a modern version has now been erected further along the dockside here for cruise liners, but it is somewhat utilitarian and does not have the splendid 'Art Deco' styling of the original building. Colour-Rail 340577

The Ocean Terminal at Southampton's Old Docks (latterly Eastern Docks) opened in 1950, with boat trains arriving there from London (Waterloo) for Berths 43 and 44 for Cunard Line services, including the *Queen Elizabeth* and *Queen Mary* liners. Boat trains from Waterloo also arrived for Berth 9 at the Continental Terminal for cross-channel destinations and the Channel Isles. Boat trains also served the New Docks (latterly Western Docks) that opened for business in phases from 1932, and contained Berths 101-108. These docks also had carriage servicing sheds and a 70ft turntable. The Union Castle Line's 'Cape' ships from South Africa used Berths 101 and 102 at the New Docks for arrivals and Berths 103 and 104 for departures. Berths 105 and 106 were for P&O ships, and Berths 107 and 108 were used by liners from other shipping lines, including United States Lines.

In the 1950s over half a million passengers used the boat trains to and from Southampton, but from the late 1950s there was a decline in the boat traffic and those using these trains, as travel by jet air-liners for trans-Atlantic journeys came to the fore, this decline stretching into the early 1960s, resulting in Southampton docks concentrating of containerised shipping.

The London & South Western Railway, who owned and managed Southampton docks, promoted fast mail ocean steamships between Southampton and all continents of the world, with special trains leaving Waterloo station for Southampton. They built new coaches for the boat trains with a pantry for supplying meals on the train, described in 1938 as kitchen cars. Later the four first-class brakes lost their pantries and were rebuilt to provide six compartments, these coaches lasting in service until 1959. In 1931 the Southern Railway introduced first-class Pullman cars for the boat trains, and by 1938 twenty of these Pullman cars were allocated to the 'Ocean Liner Express' pool.

Many regular sailings went to the Channel Isles and France from the Continental Terminal in the Old Docks, including Le Havre, from the early 1920s, and on the Friday before Whitsun in 1938 Clapham yard had to provide stock for seven boat trains. The frequency of sailings from Southampton to Le Havre was gradually reduced, and by the late 1950s they were no more than twice weekly, the trains for these sailings termed 'The Normandy Express'. The sailings to the Channel Isles from Southampton ceased in the early 1960s, this service then provided by Weymouth, and in 1964 the Southampton to Le Havre service also ceased to run.

A great deal of planning was necessary between the shipping lines, the docks division of BTC, and British Railways around six months in advance, only made possible due to the fact that Southampton was a deep water

port, meaning that ships could dock at any state of the tide, the only exceptions being *RMS Queen Mary* and the *Queen Elizabeth* that could only be dealt with a high tide. Southampton is unusual by having high tides approximately every six hours.

The Southampton docks authorities produced lists of sailings well in advance which it published each month, detailing the scheduled programme of 'Ocean Liner Trains' from Waterloo, but no list of up trains returning to London was published. The list for May 1957 is detailed in Table One of this article showing just how many destinations ships sailed to in one month, and not only does the list provide details of these locations, but also the ships used, and the departure times of boat trains for these ships from Waterloo to Southampton docks. The trains ran as 'Q paths' (run when required), and the overall timings for the boat train journeys from Waterloo to Southampton varied from 96 minutes to 110 minutes for the 80-mile journey, with around ten minutes in the dock area.

Due to the volume of boat trains running to and from Southampton the Southern Region sometimes had to borrow rolling stock from other regions. The liners docking at Southampton varied in size, but Cunard's *Queens* were some of the largest, often resulting in passengers disembarking filling three, four, or even five returning boat trains. It was a hive of activity at the docks when ships arrived and departed, and on 13 September 1957, for example, nine ocean

Table One
Scheduled 'Ocean Liner Expresses' from Waterloo — May 1957

Date	Ship	Destination	Trains departing Waterloo
2	Queen Mary	New York	8.03am, 8.54am, 9.43am
	Athlone Castle	Cape Town	9.20am, 10.20am
3	Arosa Sun	Quebec	8.10am
	Liberté	Le Havre, New York	2.45pm
4	Homeric	Le Havre, Quebec	8.27am, 9.15am
7	America	Bremerhaven, New York	9.20am
8	Mauretania	New York	8.03am, 8.54am
	Queen Elizabeth	New York (Sailing 9 May)	4.07pm, 4.43pm, 7.05pm
	Statendam	Rotterdam, New York	5.23pm
9	United States	New York	8.22am, 8.54am, 9.43am
	Carnarvon Castle	Cape Town	9.20am, 10.20am
10	Ivernia	Montreal	8.03am, 8.54am
	Ornje	Amsterdam, Djakarta	10.02am
	Ile de France	Le Havre, New York	8.40pm
16	Queen Mary	New York	8.03am, 8.54am, 9.43am
	Edinburgh Castle	Cape Town	9.20am, 10.20am
17	Arosa Sky	Bremerhaven, New York	7.05pm
18	Liberte'	Le Havre, New York	2.45pm
	Ryndam	Rotterdam, New York	5.23pm
20	Homeric	Quebec	7.05pm, 7.52pm
21	Flandre	Le Havre, New York	7.20pm
22	Nieuw Amsterdam	Rotterdam, New York	4.43pm
23	Seven Seas	Bremerhaven, Montreal	8.10am
	United States	New York	8.22am, 8.54am, 9.43am
	Winchester Castle	Cape Town	9.20am, 10.20am
	Queen Elizabeth	New York	1.20pm, 2.00pm, 2.45pm, 3.38pm
24	Alcantara	Buenos Aires	9.15am
25	Mauretania	New York	8.03am, 8.54am
	Dominion Monarch	Wellington, New Zealand	10.02am
	Muasdum	Rotterdam, New York	5.23pm
27	New York	Bremerhaven, New York	8.10am
	Ile de France	Le Havre, New York	6.22pm
29	Neptuna	Bremerhaven, Montreal	8.10am
	America	Bremerhaven, New York	9.20am
	Statendam	Rotterdam, New York	4.43pm
30	Queen Mary	New York	7.18am, 7.45am, 8.22am, 8.54am
	Corfu	Hong Kong	9.15am
	Capetown Castle	Cape Town	9.20am, 10.20am
	Southern Cross	Wellington	9.43am, 10.35am
31	Arosa Sun	Bremerhaven, Quebec	8.10am

liners docked on that day conveying 6,000 passengers; (who would have thought, at that time, that one cruise ship would one day be built to accommodate 6,000 passengers?) This situation in September 1957 resulted in twelve boat trains leaving the docks on that day, two of which were diverted to London (Victoria) to avoid congestion.

Movement of rolling stock could create big problems at times as, on occasions, empty stock trains would have to run to

This post-war aerial view of Southampton Docks shows the vast numbers of liners that called here, the land-side entrance to which had the legend 'The Gateway to the World' proudly displayed over the dock gates. The Old Docks (later renamed the Eastern Docks) are in the foreground, and the New Docks of 1935 (later renamed the Western Docks) consisting of one very long dock with multiple berths (Nos 101-108) are to the rear. Notable amongst the liners is RMS Queen Elizabeth in Berth 44 alongside the Ocean Terminal that is dead centre in the picture. Directly above her stern and berthed in the New Docks can be seen her elder sister RMS Queen Mary and, just beneath the King George V Graving Dock, their American rival, the SS United States. The key to the picture is as follows. BTC

1. Southampton (Terminus) station
2. Southampton (Central) station
3. New (or Western) Docks
4. King George V Graving Dock
5. Royal Pier
6. Town Quay
7. Trafalgar Dry Dock
8. Ocean Dock
9. Ocean Terminal
10. Empress Dock
11. Inner Dock
12. Outer Dock

The naming of the boat trains was instituted by British Railways in 1952, the first being 'The Cunarder' on 2 July of that year. Those run in connection with the ocean liners were known as Ocean Liner Expresses; there were other boat trains run in connection with cross-Channel services. Onward travel by train was still the accepted way to leave from or to return to London and the 'Queens' would generate up to five separate trains in each direction. All these would usually have two luggage vans at the front and some Pullman cars inserted in with the normal stock, all bearing colourful headboards in the Southern style. The 'Lord Nelson' class 4-6-0s became associated with the boat trains as the first eight engines of the class were allocated to Eastleigh from the start of the 1950s, being joined by three more from Bournemouth in 1956, three from Nine Elms in 1958, and the last ones, from Bournemouth, in late 1959. Here we see No 30857 *Lord Howe* at the Ocean Terminal with one of the trains for non-first-class passengers in 1956, the year second-class accommodation on British Railways was abolished. Colour-Rail BRS995

Southampton to cater for incoming ships when only one boat train would be required for outgoing passengers. Bad weather conditions at sea could also be a problem when ships arrived at Southampton late, with trains and their staff leaving for Waterloo later than intended, causing problems with scheduled passengers services between Southampton and Waterloo.

There was often an imbalance between up and down boat trains, like in 1954 when 681 boat trains left Waterloo for Southampton, but only 527 trains left the port. In July of that year as many as 87 boat trains departed from Waterloo, and there were 76 up workings. On one summer Saturday in 1953, Nine Elms and Clapham yard had to find motive power and stock for eight boat trains, in addition to stock for this peak summer Saturday. The Pullman car situation was always problematic too, as shipping companies would sell Pullman tickets to passengers on incoming sailings and would inform British Railways by wire of its

requirements, often resulting in empty trains of Pullman cars having to run from Waterloo to Southampton to meet the demand.

Many readers will recall the colourful headboards carried by the boat trains, some displaying the shipping line's name for the ship that the train was meeting, such as 'The Cunarder', in the case of that company's *Queens* ships, or 'The Statesman' for the United States Line's flagship. The name 'The South American' was for the ships of the Royal Mail Line. Others may recall colourful headboards on boat trains bearing names such as 'Greek Line' and 'Arosa Line'.

In early BR days five 8-car sets were formed for the Ocean Liner Expresses with an SR Maunsell brake composite at each end and new Bulleid-pattern open thirds and all-firsts, and from around 1954 new BR Standard open thirds and brake vehicles replaced the similar Bulleid coaches and Maunsell brake vehicles. After the Hastings route was dieselized, the Pullman cars from the Hastings steam-hauled

trains were transferred to the Southampton boat trains in 1958, and were, at first, repainted green, and in 1960 were taken into Southern Region stock, lasting until 1964. Later, even Gresley buffet cars were transferred to the Southampton boat trains to replace former Pullman buffet cars.

Regarding motive power for the Ocean Line Expresses to and from Southampton, locomotives were supplied by Nine Elms, and Eastleigh maintained a boat train link of enginemen, Eastleigh men and their locomotives called upon to work up trains that could not be balanced by Nine Elms engines and men, and in the early 1950s Eastleigh-based 'Lord Nelson' 4-6-0s were used for this purpose, all sixteen 'Lord Nelsons' being allocated to Eastleigh by 1959. Eastleigh, of course, also supplied tank engines for the shunting of boat trains in the docks, such as 'B4' class 0-4-0Ts (pre-war) and 'USA' and 'E2' class 0-6-0Ts after the war; diesel shunters took over these duties after 1963.

'The Cunarder' again, this time consisting of Pullman cars, with the exception of the first coach, a **BR Mk I** in blood & custard livery, is seen approaching the end of its up journey at Clapham Junction. The engine is 'Lord Nelson' class 4-6-0 No 30860 *Lord Hawke* working the 'Special 4' duty. The working of boat trains was always a problem as they had to meet shipping which was subject to tidal variations, and there could be an imbalance in the number of trains required. Nevertheless, it was not always necessary to stable the stock at Clapham Junction, although it was based there, other than for servicing, as the ocean liners would be set to sail relatively shortly after arrival, so many trains would work out from Southampton and back from London the same day. Stabling took place in the Western Docks where the Southern Railway had built a large carriage shed during its 1930s' expansion of the port. B. Morrison

On 15 October 1960 Eastleigh's 'Lord Nelson' 4-6-0 No 30852 *Sir Walter Raleigh* is seen hurrying through Farnborough (North) at the head of an up boat train which has no headboard, no luggage vans at the front, and boat train set No 352 comprising BR Mk I stock. The set was one of five 8-car sets which had been put together using SR Maunsell brake composites at each end and Bulleid open thirds and firsts. From 1954 onwards the original stock had been gradually replaced by new BR Mk I stock as seen here. The route indicator discs show that this train had originated in Southampton's Western Docks; a lower disc over the other buffer would indicate the origin as the Eastern Docks. In the opposite direction these indications were reversed. J.C. Beckett

The headcode discs on the boat train pictured here indicate that this train would be routed up the main line as far as Wimbledon where it would take the line across to East Putney, so that it could approach Waterloo via the Windsor lines through Clapham Junction. The train, hauled by No 30859 *Lord Hood,* is seen in Southampton Docks on Wednesday, 26 June 1957. The normal headcode would indicate a train running straight up the main line, this headcode, indicating a variation in the route, being used to indicate a non-standard path. All boat trains were scheduled to run non-stop to or from London. *R.C. Riley*

The earlier Maunsell express passenger 4-6-0s, the famous 'King Arthur' class, were often used on the Ocean Liner Expresses in their later days, as were numerous other 4-6-0s in the early 1950s. Here we see No 30773 *Sir Lavaine* at Vauxhall on 16 June 1954 at the head of the 12.39pm train to Southampton's Western Docks. The train has an ex-LMS van at the front, and the first passenger coach is one of the SR Maunsell brake composites. N. Sprinks

The goods versions of the 'N15' and 'King Arthur' 4-6-0s were often used on boat trains when demand was high for locomotives, especially the Southern-built 'S15' 4-6-0s as they were quite reasonably able to run at semi-express speeds. Some boat train timings were tight, being allowed 86 minutes from the dock gates to Waterloo, running non-stop, the same timings as was allowed the 'Bournemouth Belle' from Southampton (Central). Other boat trains, the ones usually assigned to the 'S15' 4-6-0s, were allowed 100 minutes. The 'S15' 4-6-0 pictured here near Farnborough with a down Ocean Liner Express on 20 June 1959, No 30833, was possibly the worst choice for the non-stop run as it was equipped with a 3,500 gallon 6-wheel tender, so assuming it was being thrashed to keep to time, it must have been running quite low on water when it arrived in Southampton. *J.C. Beckett*

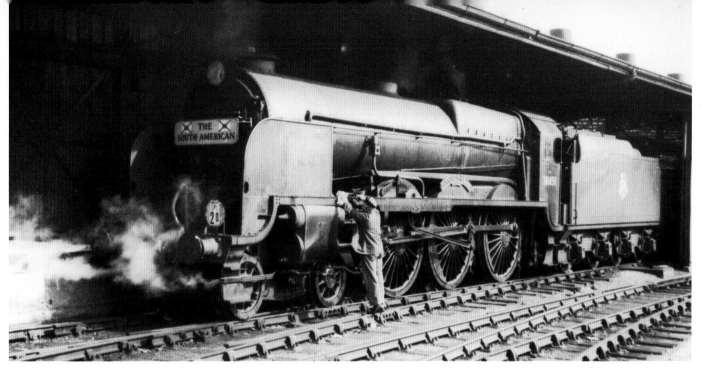

A 'Lord Nelson' class 4-6-0, No 30851 *Sir Walter Raleigh,* stands inside one of the train sheds in the Western Docks in the early 1950s at the head of a train run in connection with the sailing of a ship owned by the Royal Mail Line. The tradition of naming locomotives after almost anything to do with the sea meant that the 'Lord Nelsons' were most appropriate power for the boat trains as might have been the Bulleid 'Merchant Navy' Pacifics that honoured the shipping lines that used the port. However, the latter were seldom used on the boat trains as they had regular express diagrams, and it might have been confusing, not to say embarrassing if, say, No 35012 *United States Line* was used on 'The Cunarder'!   Lens of Sutton Collection

The earlier former L&SWR Urie 'S15' 4-6-0s were not quite as fleet of foot as their younger offsprings, but even these old war-horses sometimes had to be pressed into boat train service. On 13 August 1960 No 30508 clunked through Winchfield on a boat train for Southampton Docks with Western Section Special Traffic Set No 430, comprising ten coaches including two 1935 Maunsell brake thirds and at least five open thirds. This set would survive until the end of 1962 in this form.   J.C. Beckett

The Bulleid 'Battle of Britain' class Pacific No 34065 *Hurricane* is pictured at Waterloo on 8 October 1953 awaiting the right-away after running light into the station from Nine Elms shed wearing the headboard for the 10.20am 'Union-Castle Express', but before removal of the tail-lamp and the mounting of the indicator discs. It will probably receive one on the top lamp-bracket and one over the right-hand buffer as Union Castle ships sailed from the Western Docks. The 'H16' class 4-6-0 No 30518 is seen in the background.

Our Royal Family travelled by an all-Pullman boat train to and from Southampton at the start and conclusion of the 'Royal Tour of Commonwealth Nations', and famous people from the USA often arrived by ship at Southampton docks, such as the time when the glitzy American entertainer, Liberace, travelled to Britain in September 1956, his party being provided with its own Pullman special to London. Also, when the evangelist Billy Graham came to London, his boat docked at Southampton. During the 1950s, people from the West Indies, arriving for a new life in Britain arrived by ship at Southampton and the

army used Southampton docks when sending their troops for postings abroad.

The Pullman cars were withdrawn from the boat trains in 1963 to help cut the high costs of running the boat trains, and in January 1964, Cunard, P&O, and the Union Castle Line complained bitterly about the poor standards of cleanliness and catering on the boat trains for its passengers.

Steam-hauled boat trains continued until 1967 at the end of Southern Region steam, the final steam working being on Sunday, 9 July 1967 (the 11.00 working from Southampton docks), this train hauled by Southern Light

Pacific No 34021 *Dartmoor*. During that last week of steam operation 'Merchant Navy' Pacifics were regularly hauling boat trains to and from Southampton.

Scheduled shipping services from Southampton docks declined over the next fifteen years, and the Ocean Terminal was demolished in 1983. Now only the cruise ships arrive and depart from Southampton, generating a massive amount of business for the town as cruising becomes more popular and available to more people as cruise lines build bigger ships, proving holidays to exotic destinations for the general public at large.

One of the three long-deflector Bulleid Light Pacifics that featured in the 1948 Locomotive Exchanges, No 34006 *Bude,* is seen at the head of the 'Statesman' Ocean Liner Express approaching Clapham Junction on the down main line on 25 July 1956, to serve the *SS United States* or the *SS America* liners. This is the train for first-class passengers as it is formed of all-Pullman stock that was provided and controlled by the Pullman company that had a pool of fifty such cars available, and did not keep them in regular sets as per normal SR practice. Tickets could be booked on board incoming liners so there was a very short time available to prepare trains, and this meant that there was a great deal of marshalling of stock to form the required train capacity. B. Morrison

One of the very last Ocean Liner Expresses, running just two weeks before the end of Southern Steam on 28 June 1967, is seen speeding through Vauxhall station behind the now nameless rebuilt 'West Country' Pacific No 34013 (ex-*Okehampton*). Steam was used on most boat trains right up until the end, the final one on the last Sunday (9 July 1967) running up to Waterloo behind No 34021 (ex-*Dartmoor*). Note the condition of the locomotive — it had been used on specials and still bore some of the lustre on the buffers and smokebox door straps. The headboard was looking decidedly travel-worn! Following the cessation of these trains the boards were stored in a hut at Eastleigh Works and survived many clearouts. Most of them are now the prized possessions of steam-era collectors. G.F. Bloxham/Colour-Rail 343222

Access to the Eastern Docks was made over the famous Canute Road level crossing that was situated next to the South Western Hotel that was built by the L&SWR and was an integral part of Southampton (Terminus) station. In the last days the boat trains were worked by whatever locomotives were available, and on 9 June 1967 a BR Standard '4MT' Mogul, No 76064, was entrusted with a short boat train, and is seen leaving Southampton Docks. J. Bird/Platform 14 J8643

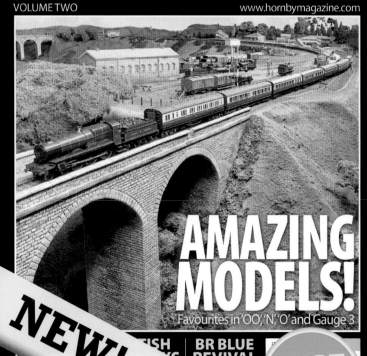

The Giesl 'Spam-Cans'

Andrew Wilson *recalls the last major modification to an unrebuilt Southern Light Pacific, the fitting of a Giesl ejector to No 34064* Fighter Command, *and its later adoption on No 34092* City of Wells.

The 'Battle of Britain' class Light Pacific, No 34064 *Fighter Command*, works a down express to Bournemouth past Durnsford Road power station, Wimbledon, on 18 July 1964, whilst also passing BR Standard '4MT' 4-6-0 No 75078 on the down slow line. The Giesl ejector is less prominent than the usual Bulleid 'dust bin' chimney fitted to the remaining unmodified Southern Light Pacifics. The light hazy exhaust is evidence of good combustion in the firebox and high superheating of the steam. 340493/Colour-Rail.com

The daily journey to grammar school in Battersea High Street necessitated a change of bus at Clapham Junction, and so there were few days when a visit by me to the platforms was not made. When cycling to school was permitted, a diversion up Battersea Rise provided the perfect grandstand to see what was happening on the Brighton and Woking lines in Clapham Junction cutting. It was here that I first saw Southern 'Battle of Britain' class Light Pacific No 34064 *Fighter Command* heading west in charge of a down Bournemouth express after its last general repair at Eastleigh Works in April 1962. The date would have been September 1964, and I couldn't believe my eyes as the usual 'Spam-Can' dustbin-shaped chimney had gone, replaced by a long thin vent. Of course nobody at school believed a word.

When completed at Brighton Works in July 1947 as Southern Railway No 21C164 this Light Pacific locomotive was credited with being the 1,000th locomotive to built at the former LB&SCR Works. When it emerged nameless from the erecting shops it was finished in workshop grey livery, and after being steamed and given a test run in went back into the paint shops and was painted in Bulleid's eye-catching malachite green, lined out with three broad parallel yellow lines that ran from the front of the engine to the rear of the tender. After the decision was made to

name No 21C164 *Fighter Command* it would be 11 September 1947 before the nameplates and RAF plaques were ceremoniously unveiled at Waterloo station by Air Chief Marshal Sir James Robb.

As with all the Light Pacifics, No 34064 underwent a number of modifications, the first being the immediate fitting of a wedge-shaped cab, and in June 1948 it received a standard 3-window cab arrangement. In June 1948 a repaint into an experimental apple green livery with lining at the top and bottom of the air-smoothed casing and tender, and the legend BRITISH RAILWAYS on the tender, was authorised; the standard dark green British Railways livery was applied in June 1950. In July 1953 a new middle cylinder was fitted, and two years later the boiler pressure was reduced from 280psi to 250psi. New crank pins were fitted in March 1956, but it was not until August 1960 that a speedometer and AWS equipment were fitted.

When first released to traffic, No 21C164 was allocated to Ramsgate shed for use on the important Kent coast workings. At the beginning of the second week of January 1949 it was transferred to Stewarts Lane depot, but in the middle of March 1950 it was moved across London to Nine Elms shed where it was employed on services to Bournemouth, Salisbury, Weymouth, and Exeter. It remained at Nine Elms until transferred to Exmouth Junction in June 1959, but May 1962 saw it returned to Nine Elms. Moved to Eastleigh in January 1964, a final transfer to Salisbury came in October 1965 from where it worked out its final seven months in traffic.

The Southern Bulleid Light Pacifics in their original form were well known for their fire-throwing propensities. I vividly remember watching 'West Country' Pacific No 34002 *Salisbury* working hard through Clapham Junction cutting after replacing Gresley 'V2' class 2-6-2 No 60919 at short notice on the LCGB's 'Green Arrow' special on Sunday, 3 July 1966, and setting fire to the up side of the embankment.

Attempts to fit spark arresters had a detrimental effect on the Bulleid Pacific's free-steaming qualities. The problem was that the Lemaître multiple-jet exhaust could not be made to produce enough draft to overcome the extra resistance to gas flow through the boiler caused by the spark arrester plates or mesh. Sharpening the blast did not solve the problem, but did cause a reduction in power output.

In 1958 Dr Gieslingen approached the British Railways Board to offer a free trial of his ejector with a view to achieving economies in coal consumption and boiler efficiencies. When this was turned down he made the same offer to the Talyllyn Railway, and they agreed to allow him to convert 0-4-2T *Edward Thomas*. Initially a coal-saving in the order of 40% was claimed, but later this was rescinded, and after 1969, when the ejector was removed, it was claimed that it has made little or no difference to the performance of *Edward Thomas*. In June 1960, however, BR Standard '9F' class 2-10-0 No 92250 was also fitted with a Giesl oblong ejector. The design of the '9F' locomotive, however, was so good that the ejector had little or no effect on its performance or coal consumption.

Brand-new 'Battle of Britain' class Light Pacific No 21C164 has been outshopped in workshop grey livery and stands outside Brighton Works in July 1947. Reckoned to be the 1,000th locomotive built at the former LB&SCR Works, No 21C164 has the original style of cab that was quickly replaced by a wedge-shaped one to improve the forward vision of the footplate crew. The radical appearance of the Bulleid Pacifics was softened somewhat by the eye-catching malachite green and yellow livery used by the Southern Railway. W. Beckerlegge/Rail Archive Stephenson

At Eastleigh Works, John Click, the Assistant Works Manager, thought that the Giesl ejector might finally overcome the Light Pacific's spark-arresting problem. In theory, the ejector's greater efficiency compared with the Lemaître multiple-jet exhaust arrangement ought to overcome the resistance caused by the mesh of a spark arrester without affecting the steaming of the boiler, but with the advantage of reducing the back-pressure on the pistons. The ejector itself had seven nozzles, effectively seven correctly-shaped chimneys rolled into one, with blower jets placed between them, arranged in line to exhaust into a narrow chimney around which a hinged fine wire-mesh spark arrester was fitted. With the chimney fixed in perfect alignment with the blast pipe, one cause of poor steaming was immediately eliminated.

The chimney was also made into three sections and could simply be removed for access to the superheater tubes and then replaced with the alignment unaltered. With the Giesl ejector the exhaust leaves the chimney top with much greater velocity, and this, combined with the narrow frontal area of the chimney, also made a great improvement to the smoke lifting of these locomotives than any of the earlier alterations made to the smoke deflectors.

To use the Giesl ejector, British Railways had to pay a license fee, and with steam's

A little over two months after its last general repair at Eastleigh Works, when the Giesl ejector was fitted, No 34064 *Fighter Command*, both engine and tender, have lost their ex-paint shop finish. The Light Pacific is seen near Sway on Saturday, 16 June 1962 in charge of a Waterloo to Bournemouth excursion. As can be seen, the Giesl ejector is lifting the exhaust well clear of the air-smoothed casing and cab. D.M.C. Hepburne-Scott/Rail Archive Stephenson

On Saturday, 28 September 1963 No 34064 *Fighter Command* climbs from West Wycombe towards Saunderton when in charge of the Talyllyn Railway Society AGM Special from Paddington to Towyn via Shrewsbury, Ruabon, and Morfa Mawddach. The Giesl ejector is working well in lifting the exhaust clear of the cab. The Western Region crew, however, struggled to cope with the idiosyncrasies of the Light Pacific, and arrival at Shrewsbury was an hour late and, as a result, 1963 was the last year a Talyllyn Railway AGM Special used a Southern Region locomotive. Brian Stephenson

future prospects short-term at best, this was reason enough not to fit any further Southern Light Pacifics with the ejector. The original idea had been to fit the ejectors to forty of the unconverted Light Pacifics and to twenty of the rebuilds, but at £500 a time such an outlay could not be countenanced. The choice of No 34064 *Fighter Command* was down to serendipity as it was simply the next unrebuilt Light Pacific waiting at Eastleigh Works in

March 1962 for a general repair. The ejector was manufactured in Austria, and initially it was over-draughted because Dr Gieslingen had not taken into account the Light Pacific's lack of dampers, despite John Click making a specific request for the Austrians to be careful not to overdraft the ejector.

At the end of April, *Fighter Command* was ready for testing, and after the usual steam tests it was ready for road-testing on 3 May

1962. There were a number of teething problems because of the modified draughting that caused the brick arch to burn away along with the superheater ends. The steel fire hole rim protector also melted, but with these problems solved by nothing more than relatively minor adjustments to the height of the blast pipe, and with the nozzles increased in size, No 34064 was released back into normal traffic.

The 'Battle of Britain' class Light Pacific No 34064 *Fighter Command* has just passed Weybridge in charge of a Waterloo to Bournemouth express on Thursday, 30 April 1964. When viewed from this angle the Giesl chimney is difficult to distinguish, but there is no doubting the efficiency of the exhaust, as the expelled steam and smoke is a light grey in colour. The stains on the air-smoothed casing are the result of a boiler wash-out and the chemicals used at Nine Elms shed to soften the hard London water. D.M.C. Hepburne-Scott/Rail Archive Stephenson

Seen from the vantage point of Battersea Rise road bridge, the narrow elongated chimney of No 34064 is clearly seen. After negotiating the speed restriction through Clapham Junction station on Saturday, 30 May 1964 in charge of the heavy 12-coach 11.30am Waterloo to Bournemouth train, the driver of *Fighter Command* has opened up the Light Pacific, yet the exhaust is just a light haze. Brian Stephenson

All the top-link firemen at Nine Elms shed, where No 34064 was now allocated, were given a handout explaining the principles of the ejector, and what to expect. Just how many read the booklet is a moot point, but *Fighter Command* soon gained a reputation as the best Southern Light Pacific in original form. I remember going to a RCTS meeting to hear Bert Hooker speak, and he said that No 34064 was transformed into the best Light Pacific he had driven, almost the equivalent of a good 'Merchant Navy' class Pacific, but more susceptible to slipping, but was now capable of passing Clapham Junction in less than the seven minutes allowed for most of the down West of England expresses.

The bane of many Nine Elms firemen's lives was a tender full of the dreaded briquettes (coal dust mixed with cement). Even with this fuel No 34064 would steam freely, albeit with the tender becoming depleted rapidly as the fireman bent his back. Another Bert Hooker memory of *Fighter Command* was of it working a down two-hour express from Waterloo to Bournemouth. Booking on at Vauxhall, No 34064 was waiting at Waterloo at the head of thirteen coaches. The tender was a mixture of coal and

briquettes, yet the boiler pressure hovered around the 240psi mark for most of the trip, and Clapham Junction was easily passed in the scheduled seven minutes from Waterloo, while the 28 miles between Southampton (Central) and Bournemouth were covered in even time, feats rarely achieved by Southern Light Pacifics in original condition.

My first run behind No 34064 came on Saturday, 28 September 1963 when it worked train Z85, the Talyllyn Railway's AGM special between Paddington and Ruabon via Shrewsbury. The load was nine Southern Region Bulleid corridor coaches, some 286tons tare,

300tons loaded. Manned by a Western Region crew with a Southern Region inspector, *Fighter Command* made hard work of getting away from Paddington, slipping furiously as the driver struggled to master the unfamiliar regulator and unpredictable steam reverser. Already running behind time through Greenford, things picked up on the down gradient towards Princes Risborough after a competent climb of Saunderton bank. By Banbury the train was some thirty minutes late, and after climbing Hatton bank without any undue alarms the special rolled into Birmingham (Snow Hill) station 35 minutes late.

Standing pilot at Staines for the funeral train of Sir Winston Churchill on Saturday, 30 January 1965 No 34064 *Fighter Command* has been cleaned to perfection. Now fitted with AWS equipment, the battery box can be seen above the front buffer beam and Giesl ejector and, these apart, No 34064 is in the final form of the unmodified Light Pacifics when coupled to a cut-down tender.

The Giesl ejector made for 'West Country' Light Pacific No 34092 *City of Wells*, identical to that fitted to No 34064, is seen prior to being installed. As can be seen, the ejector has seven nozzles, or blast pipes, in line with the blower jets placed between them. The substantial brackets at each end were attached to the chimney to ensure perfect alignment and draughting. John Sagar

A pedestrian run to Wolverhampton resulted in the train leaving some 45 minutes late. A workmanlike run to Shrewsbury was spoilt by a signal check on the Abbey Curve alongside the Severn Bridge Junction signal box as there was no platform available. When the signal cleared, No 34064 was unable to restart the train, and Ivatt '2MT' 2-6-2T No 41209 had to be commandeered to bank the train into the station. After handing over to BR-built 'Manors' Nos 7827 *Lydham Manor* and 7822 *Foxcote Manor*, No 34064 retired to Shrewsbury shed for servicing. For the return trip some sleeping cars had been attached to the train at Machynlleth, and No 34064 eventually arrived back at Paddington in the early hours of Sunday morning, having been halted near Shifnal by a passenger pulling the communication cord.

My only other run behind *Fighter Command* came during the following summer when travelling from Bournemouth to Waterloo. With thirteen coaches, some 450tons tare and 480tons full, this load would have been a difficult one for a 'Merchant Navy' Pacific, let alone a Light Pacific with the

continuous 1 in 250 gradient from St. Denys to Litchfield tunnel. The crew was obviously up for the challenge as the 28.8miles from Bournemouth (Central) to Southampton (Central) were covered in 29 minutes, with a top speed of 79mph through Beaulieu Road. The 12½miles to Winchester (City) station took just seventeen minutes, while the 72-minute schedule for the 66½miles to Waterloo was run in just 69 minutes, despite signal checks outside Surbiton and Clapham Junction.

For the funeral train of Sir Winston Churchill on Saturday, 30 January 1965, *Fighter Command* was brought up to Nine Elms shed from Eastleigh where it joined Light Pacifics Nos 34051 *Winston Churchill* and 34057 *Biggin Hill* to be prepared for a part in this prestigious duty. No 34051 was selected to work the special, with No 34057 the standby locomotive at Nine Elms. No 34064 was sent to Staines to stand pilot in case of problems with No 34051. In the event, *Fighter Command* was not needed, and was later worked back to Eastleigh where it resumed its normal duties.

When due for a heavy repair in May 1966 the decision to stop overhauling the non-modified Light Pacifics had been made, and so on 22 May of that year No 34064 was withdrawn after running an estimated 759,666miles. Of these, approximately 176,000 had been run since the fitting of the Giesl ejector. Whether the full benefits of the ejector were fully realised is a moot point, but the withdrawal of *Fighter Command* was not an end to the story of the Light Pacifics and the Giesl ejector as in 1985 the preserved 'West Country' class Pacific No 34092 *City of Wells* was fitted with an identical ejector to that used on No 34064 *Fighter Command*.

The complete Giesl ejector and chimney is now ready for installing in the smokebox of No 34092. Once securely fitted, a hinged fine wire-mesh spark arrester was fitted around the chimney. Until the advent of the Giesl ejector, the draughting of steam locomotives had always been a question of trial and error, and the effect this relatively cheap modification made to the performance of both Nos 34064 and 34092 was remarkable, but it came too late in the day for steam on British Railways. John Sagar

This smokebox view of No 34092 shows the Giesl ejector and spark arrester in situ, and also illustrates the layout of the front tube-plate, steam pipes, and superheater elements in both Nos 34064 and 34092. The fine char collected at the bottom of the smokebox still had to be shovelled out by a shed labourer — one of the more unpopular tasks involved with disposing a steam locomotive. John Sagar

The Worth Valley Railway-based No 34092 returned to the main line on 12 December 1981 working the SLOA 'Golden Arrow' between Carnforth and Hellifield in Arctic weather conditions. No 34092 *City of Wells* proved to be a more than competent performer, steaming well and capable of handling heavy loads. One problem that was commented on by most of the footplate crews and inspectors was the old bugbear of drifting smoke and the insufficient lifting of the exhaust over the cab. Backing this up, I recall seeing *City of Wells* climbing through Ribblehead station at the head of the SLOA 'Cumbrian Mountain Pullman' in appalling weather conditions with all but the smokebox front shrouded in steam and smoke.

As a result, the decision was taken to fit No 34092 with a Giesl ejector, identical to that used on No 34064. This brought about the desired effect, with improved fuel economy, better lifting of the exhaust, and higher power outputs. Such was the improvement that *City of Wells* has produced some 1,900edhp, thereby all but equalling the record for the class of 2,010edhp set by 'West Country' Pacific No 34006 *Bude* during the Locomotive Exchanges of 1948. Given that *Bude* was running with the boiler working at 280psi rather than the 250psi of No 34092, there is little if anything to chose between the power outputs.

The National Coal Board also fitted at least 25 of its 'Austerity' 0-6-0STs with Giesl ejectors, but it was the modifications to No 34064, and later No 34092, that showed the potential of the ejector. If Southern Region steam had been phased out during 1970/71 it is possible that a significant number of the Bulleid Light Pacifics would have been given Giesl ejectors.

'The decision was taken to fit No 34092 with a Giesl ejector, identical to that used on No 34064. This brought about the desired effect, with improved fuel economy, better lifting of the exhaust, and higher power outputs. Such was the improvement that City of Wells *has produced some 1,900edhp, thereby all but equalling the record for the class of 2,010edhp set by 'West Country' Pacific No 34006* Bude *during the Locomotive Exchanges of 1948. Given that* Bude *was running with the boiler working at 280psi rather than the 250psi of No 34092, there is little if anything to chose between the power outputs.'*

The 'West Country' class Light Pacific No 34092 *City of Wells* is seen in Haworth yard on the Worth Valley Railway on Sunday, 14 September 1986 on the visit of Dr Gieslingen, inventor of the Giesl ejector exhaust system. From left to right are John Click, John Adams, Richard Greenwood, Dr Gieslingen, and Graham Bentley. H. Blackie/KWVR Archives

Giesl-fitted No 34092 *City of Wells* in charge of the 15.35 Sheffield to Marylebone 'South Yorkshireman' railtour as it takes the Derby route at Clay Cross South Junction on Saturday 21 May 1988. A sweltering hot day masks just how hard the engine is working, but already five minutes of a 16-late start had been made up. Roger Smith

STEAM DAYS

In Colour

The Southern's 'Withered Arm'

The Southern lines west of Exeter took on the appearance of a 'withered arm' on a map. That metaphor unfortunately also became the reality between 1966 and 1970 as the network was decimated by successive line closures. The last railway had arrived on the scene as late as 1925 when the Halwill & Torrington Railway line opened for business. Like many of these West Country routes it was built to tap into the area's rich mineral resources, but was also the beneficiary of the Southern's integrated approach to passenger timetabling that also made the most of the brief but lucrative summer holiday business.

At Exeter (St. David's) station on Saturday, 4 April 1959, former L&SWR 'T9' 4-4-0 No 30726 gets underway with the 3.48pm Exeter (Central) to Okehampton all-stations stopper. Here, as at Plymouth (North Road), the Great Western and Southern trains from London passed each other going in opposite directions, and an uneasy peace was sustained between the two over the joint operations agreed between here and Cowley Bridge Junction just over a mile away, north of Exeter, where the two routes diverged. Peter W. Gray

Southern Maunsell 'N' class Mogul No 31848, with the 3.14pm Ilfracombe to Barnstaple Junction goods, nears Barnstaple junction station with a reasonable load of vans on Monday, 26 August 1963. The plug was pulled on Ilfracombe line goods services from the start of the winter timetable, 7 September 1964, with North Cornwall line freight going at the same time. On the left, the roof of Barnstaple town station is just visible above the sheds of the Devon concrete works, which was rail connected via a convoluted link to the Torrington line behind the cameraman. Curiously a former BR Wickham inspection trolley, No B238W, latterly found a home here as a works shunter. Peter W. Gray

Ilfracombe generated a considerable level of seasonal holiday traffic, with most of these passenger workings banked or double-headed out of the resort. On Saturday, 13 July 1963 the 8.35am Ilfracombe to Manchester (Exchange) train, made up of former LMS coaching stock, is seen climbing the final few yards of the 1 in 36 bank before the grade eases on the approach to Mortehoe station. The two Exmouth Junction-allocated Bulleid Light Pacifics, 'West Country' class No 34020 *Seaton* piloting 'Battle of Britain' class No 34066 *Spitfire*, have their steam sanders on and safety valves lifting, with no sign of slipping. Rebuilt Light Pacifics were barred west of Exeter, but were eventually allowed to venture beyond on the main line to Plymouth only. This limitation did however mean that there was a requirement for unmodified examples for duties such as this. T.B. Owen/Colour-Rail 392336

With the line to Barnstaple and Ilfracombe visible in the distance, BR Standard '5MT' 4-6-0 No 73162 has just passed Coleford Junction with the 11.45am Exeter (Central) to Plymouth (North Road) service on Saturday, 20 June 1964. This was an all-stations stopper that followed the Surbiton to Okehampton car carrier train, taking 127 minutes to cover the 59¼-mile journey. This route reached the highest point of the Southern, at 950ft above sea level, between Meldon and Bridestowe. By contrast, the Great Western route between the two cities was 6½miles shorter, but trains paid the price of having to contend with the notorious South Devon banks each side of Totnes at Dainton and Rattery. Peter W. Gray

Former L&SWR 'T9' class 4-4-0 No 30717 is turned at Okehampton shed on Tuesday, 14 July 1959. The Southern renewed most of the facilities here over the years with this 70ft turntable replacing a 50ft example in 1947. The shed itself was a sub-shed of Exmouth Junction, but the original single-road wooden structure burnt down in 1920 and was replaced a few months later with one constructed of concrete blocks, and with an asbestos roof; clearly this one wasn't going to go up in smoke in a hurry! R.C. Riley

The L&SWR main line beyond Lydford entered Plymouth from the west via the Plymouth, Devonport & South Western Junction Railway and ran through the city to terminate on the east side at Plymouth (Friary) station. On Tuesday, 17 June 1958, 'M7' class 0-4-4Ts Nos 30035 and 30034 await their next duties at Plymouth (Friary) depot. When the BR regional boundaries were re-aligned, the shed was transferred to the Western Region from 23 February 1958. From 15 September of that year the nearby Friary station closed and Southern services were curtailed at Plymouth (North Road), which was in the process of a major rebuild. By this time Friary depot was home to just twenty locomotives, all used on local duties. These were four Drewry diesel shunters interloped with four Ivatt 2-6-2Ts, three ex-L&SWR 'B4' 0-4-0Ts, one ex-L&SWR 'G6,' 0-6-0T, four ex-L&SWR 'O2' 0-4-4Ts, and four ex-L&SWR 'M7' class 0-4-4Ts, Nos 30034-37 that were employed on the eight short return workings to Tavistock (North) and on empty stock workings, duties also shared with the Ivatt tanks. No 30037 was soon withdrawn by the Western Region in May 1958, and in February 1960 No 30035 was swapped for Ivatt 2-6-2T No 41310, but the other two 'M7s' lingered on. W. Potter/Kidderminster Railway Museum

On a September Saturday in 1959, 'T9' class 4-4-0 No 30715 has slowed to comply with the 15mph speed limit over bridge No 153 at Little Petherick Creek as its train nears journey's end at Padstow. This is the North Cornwall portion of 7.30am train from Waterloo that was split at Halwill Junction, with the other section going to Bude. The train had previously split at Exeter (Central) with the other half serving North Devon. The 'T9' 4-4-0 would turn on the 70ft turntable at the terminus and return with the 3.13pm passenger and perishables train to Okehampton.
Derek Cross/Colour-Rail BRS257

At Bude, BR Standard '3MT' 2-6-2T No 82023 readies the stock for the 5.32pm train to Halwill Junction on Saturday, 16 June 1962. In the main platform are through coaches from the 11.00am service from Waterloo that had arrived at 4.16pm behind Maunsell 'N' class Mogul No 31406. The following weekend the full onslaught on the summer timetable kicked in, with through trains to and from the capital stretching the modest facilities available here. The 'Atlantic Coast Express' departed from Bude at 11.45am on summer Saturdays, with reciprocal services departing from Waterloo at 10.35am and 11.15am. The later train returned from Bude at 9.45pm on Sundays. R.C. Riley

The Southern perfected the art of timetabling, and whilst it was not always possible or appropriate to introduce a regular-interval service, great effort was made to provide through coaches and connecting services. No more was this apparent than at Halwill Junction. Three connecting services are in sight in this June 1962 view, with Maunsell 'N' class Mogul No 31835 departing at 10.47am with a North Cornwall line service to Padstow. BR '3MT' 2-6-2T No 82010 is waiting to drop on to the Bude portion of the train that will get underway at 10.50am, whilst the crew of the 10.52am train to Torrington waits for all the excitement to subside before ambling off with Ivatt 2-6-2T No 41294 and a single Bulleid brake composite. Peter W. Gray/Colour-Rail BRS434

Former L&SWR 'O2' class 0-4-4T No 30236 arrives at Bodmin (North) with the 2.52pm train from Padstow on Whit Monday, 18 May 1959. A pair of 'O2s' were allocated to Wadebridge after World War I and quickly found favour on Bodmin (North) services, pushing aside a regular turn previously in the hands of Adams Radial 4-4-2Ts Nos 050, 054, 0169, and 0522. Their deployment proved to be a wise decision as the 'O2s' saw over forty years of use on this service before a surplus of Western Region 0-6-0PTs, looking for work, stole the duty. No 30236 was one of two 'O2' 0-4-4Ts at Wadebridge, and there were another four at Plymouth that were employed on Callington branch services, local pilot, and goods duties that were transferred to the Western Region on 23 February 1958 when regional boundary changes pushed the former L&SWR lines west of Wilton the same way. Michael Mensing

On Tuesday, 19 July 1960, Beattie '0298' class 2-4-0WT No 30585 shunts at Wenfordbridge, the isolated terminus of the 6-mile goods-only line from Dunmere Junction on the Bodmin & Wadebridge Railway. These locomotives began life working busy urban passenger trains in and out of the capital but ended up just about as far away from that as was possible, for at 266 miles this was the furthest point of the Southern's network from Waterloo. A privately-owned railway had once continued on beyond here to serve De Land quarries via a steep gravity-worked incline until operations ceased in 1940. Opened in 1834, the L&SWR illegally acquired the Bodmin & Wadebridge Railway in 1847, but it remained isolated from the rest of the company's network until 1895 when the North Cornwall Railway opened. This isolation inadvertently led to the survival of these diminutive yet powerful locomotives, but ultimately they were found to be the only engines suitable for this lightly-laid and sharply-curved mineral line. R.C. Riley

The Southern Region's last steam sheds

On New Year's Day 1948, the Southern Region had sixty steam sheds, this number reducing to nine, nineteen years later, all of which were in terminal decline, as **Andrew Wilson** *recalls.*

The Southern Railway passed on sixty steam sheds to the Southern Region of British Railways on New Year's Day 1948 *(see Table One, see page 78)*. These ranged from the large depots at Nine Elms and Exmouth Junction to the small single-road sheds at Swanage and Lyme Regis, and those at Newport and Ryde on the Isle of Wight. Within weeks of nationalisation New Cross Gate shed had lost its last engines to become a stabling point and storage point for withdrawn locomotives. Electrification and the decision to rid the Southern Region of steam traction by mid-1967 saw the region reduced to just nine steam sheds on 1 January 1967, two of which were reduced to signing-on and servicing points, with no allocation of their own *(see Table Two, page 78)*.

Ryde (Isle of Wight)

The first engine shed closure of 1967 was on the Isle of Wight at Ryde (coded 70H). Since the demise of Newport (70G) in November 1957 the island's allocation of tank engines was allocated to Ryde. The first shed was built by the Isle of Wight Railway in 1864 to the south of St. John's station and was replaced in 1874 by a two-road through shed on the opposite of side of the station, the original shed becoming part of the Works. The years

An atmospheric night scene at Ryde shed, captured on film towards the end of 1966, finds no less than six of the island's Adams 'O2' class 0-4-4Ts in light steam in the company of the resident diesel shunter No D2554, a Hunslet 0-6-0 diesel-mechanical 204hp shunter. The shed yard is in typical condition for the end of steam, with piles of ash and clinker littering the walkways between the tracks. One 'O2' 0-4-4T, No W24 *Calbourne*, is now preserved, and was bought for £900 to work on the embryonic Isle of Wight Steam Railway. *Edwin Wilmshurst*

Two of the 'O2' class 0-4-4Ts that remained active until the end of December 1966, Nos W17 *Seaview* and W22 *Brading*, are seen inside Ryde engine shed as the sands of time run out for the Isle of Wight steam services. Both engines have lost their cast nameplates but are carrying hand-painted replicas, and are in a cared-for condition, despite the imminent threat of redundancy hanging over most of the shed's staff. The December 1891-built No W17 arrived on the island in May 1930, and the June 1892-built No W22 left the mainland in June 1924. *Edwin Wilmshurst*

The last rites of steam on the Isle of Wight were played out on Saturday, 31 December 1966, and 'O2' 0-4-4T No W14, the one-time *Fishbourne*, is being prepared for its final day in service on Ryde shed. Carrying a 'Farewell to IoW Steam' headboard, an attempt is being made to clean up the paintwork. Built at Nine Elms Works in December 1889 and transferred to the island in May 1936, the 76-year-old veteran would soon be laid up awaiting scrapping at Newport. Colour-Rail 392040

gradually took their toll of the structure and in 1930 the Southern Railway provided a new two-road through depot to the east, constructed of asbestos sheeting on a steel framework, some of which had seen service as girders for the LB&SCR's overhead electrification scheme.

In 1950 Ryde shed's allocation stood at twelve 'O2' class 0-4-4Ts, Nos W14-W25, while Newport was home to 'E1' class 0-6-0Ts Nos W1-W4 and 'O2' class 0-4-4Ts Nos W26-W36, a total of fifteen tank engines. Newport's demise came about because of the gradual closure of the island's western lines. In 1966, under the recommendations of the Beeching Report, services were withdrawn on the Ryde to Newport and Cowes lines, and between Shanklin and Ventnor, leaving only the Ryde to Shanklin line intact, albeit under threat of closure.

Despite these closures, Ryde was still home to fourteen 'O2' class 0-4-4Ts, Nos W14, W16, W17, W20-W22, W24, W26-W29, W31, W33, and W35 in January 1966. This was reduced by four with the withdrawal of Nos W21, W26, W29, and W35 during the year, leaving ten of the 0-4-4Ts to see steam out on the island on 31 December 1966, along with the resident diesel shunter, No D2554.

Two 'O2' class 0-4-4-Ts, Nos W24 and W31, were retained for working engineering trains in conjunction with the electrification of the Ryde to Shanklin line, and these engines were withdrawn in March 1967. The last 'O2' class 0-4-4T to be steamed, however, was No W27 at Newport on 18 April 1967, when it shunted the withdrawn 0-4-4Ts for the scrap merchant. For a number of years the old steam shed was used as a wagon repair shop, but as what little goods traffic remaining dwindled away the wagon shop was closed, and inevitably the shed was demolished.

Table Two
Southern Region Steam Sheds, 1 January 1967

Nine Elms 70A; Feltham*; Guildford 70C; Basingstoke*; Eastleigh 70D; Salisbury 70E; Bournemouth 70F Weymouth 70G; Ryde (IoW) 70H.

* By 1967 Feltham and Basingstoke had no allocation, but were in use as servicing and signing-on points, both Feltham and Basingstoke sheds closing to steam at the end of the first week of July 1967.

Table One
Southern Region Steam Sheds, 1 January 1948

Eastern & Central Divisions

Ashford	AFD	Gillingham	GIL	Tonbridge	TON
Canterbury West	CAN	New Cross Gate	NX	Tunbridge Wells West	TWW
Bricklayers Arms	BA	Norwood Jn	NOR		
Hither Green	HIT	Ramsgate	RAM		
Brighton	BTN	Redhill	RED		
Newhaven	NHN	St. Leonards	St. L		
Dover Marine	DOV	Eastbourne	EBN		
Folkestone Jn	FOL	Stewarts Lane	BAT		

Western Division

Basingstoke	BAS	Exmouth Jn	EXJ	Feltham	FEL
Bournemouth Central	BM	Seaton	SEA	Fratton	FRA
Swanage	SWE	Lyme Regis	LR	Gosport	GOS
Hamworthy Jn	HAM	Exmouth	EXM	Midhurst	MID
Dorchester	DOR	Okehampton	OKE	Guildford	GFD
Weymouth	WEY	Bude	BUD	Bordon	BOR
Eastleigh	ELH	Launceston	LCN	Ash	ASH
Winchester	WIN	Plymouth Friary	PLY	Horsham	HOR
Southampton	SOT	Callington	CAL	Bognor	BOG
Lymington	LYM	Wadebridge	WAD	Three Bridges	3B
Andover Jn	AND	Barnstaple	BPL	Nine Elms	9E
		Torrington	TOR	Reading	RDG
		Ilfracombe	ILF	Salisbury	SAL
				Yeovil	YEO
				Templecombe	TEM

Isle of Wight

Newport	NPT	Ryde	RYD

Feltham shed in 1967 was a shadow of its former self, and here we find one of the Southern Region's surviving BR Standard '4MT' 2-6-4Ts in steam outside the shed. The last steam engines allocated to the shed were four of these 2-6-4Ts, and two of them, Nos 80085 and 80140, were transferred to Nine Elms and not condemned until the end of the first week of July 1967. Ian Krause/Kidderminster Railway Museum 187643

Feltham

Feltham engine shed opened shortly after the Grouping in 1923, but its origins can be traced back to the early days of the 20th century when the L&SWR was expanding its locomotive and goods facilities and developing a new hump shunting yard on a green-field site at Feltham. The new engine shed at Feltham saw the closure of the large Strawberry Hill (Fulwell Junction) depot as well as the smaller engine sheds at Kingston on Thames and Richmond. When Feltham shed was at full compliment it employed 350 men of whom 234 were footplatemen. The locomotive allocation of around eighty was mostly freight types, and for many years it housed more 'S15' class 4-6-0s than any other Southern Railway depot. The shed's L&SWR origins, however, ensured that it had a representative collection of the company's mixed traffic and goods engines. Two locomotive classes, however, were designed and constructed specifically for Feltham — the Urie 'G16' 4-8-0Ts and 'H16' 4-6-2Ts.

Having been the Southern Railway and Southern Region's principal freight shed in London, handling cross-London freights and long-distance workings to the south-west of England, the loss of goods services to road transport, and dieselisation, brought about a rapid decline in the 1950s and early 1960s. The 350hp 0-6-0 diesel-electric shunters saw the demise of the 'G16' 4-8-0Ts, and the 'H16' Pacific tanks were usurped by the 'Type 2' and 'Type 3' Bo-Bo diesel electric locomotives. Such was the speed of the transition that by the middle of 1965 Feltham was left with only a handful of steam duties that included a goods working to Nine Elms yard and another to Kingston. The repair shop, however, was kept busy, carrying out running repairs to the dwindling number of steam locomotives still at work. Feltham shed lost its last allocation of steam locomotives in October 1966 when BR '4MT' 2-6-4Ts Nos 80085 and 80140 were transferred to Nine Elms, and Nos 80033 and 80068 were withdrawn.

Feltham shed remained open as a servicing, repair, and signing-on point until the end of Southern Region steam, by which time the 'Type 3' Bo-Bo diesels had been joined by the 'E6000' electro-diesels. My last visit to the shed was on 3 June 1967 when I found just four steam locomotives — 'West Country' Pacific No 34047 and three BR Standard locomotives, Nos 75058, 80154, and 82019. Plans to convert the shed into a diesel depot came to nothing, and the shed was eventually demolished.

Basingstoke

Opened in 1905 by the L&SWR, Basingstoke's principal function was as a servicing point for cross-country freights, but it was also responsible for a number of local services and some semi-fast trains to and from Waterloo. In L&SWR and Southern Railway days it always had a pilot in steam round the clock, and in the 1930s this was often an Adams 4-4-0 locomotive. On 21 May 1949 Basingstoke shed's allocation stood at 23, comprising one 'G6' 0-6-0T, two 'T9' 4-4-0s, two '700' class 0-6-0s, two 'L12' 4-4-0s, two 'N15' 4-6-0s, four 'U' class 2-6-0s, two 'E1'

On an unrecorded date in the summer of 1966 three BR Standard '5MT' 4-6-0s, Nos 73119, 73118, and 73020, await their next duty outside Basingstoke shed which had lost its last allocation of steam locomotives in March 1963. No 73119 was allocated to Eastleigh, No 73118 to Guildford, and No 73020 to Weymouth at the time. All three 4-6-0s were withdrawn in 1967, No 73119 in the March, and Nos 73118 and 73020 in July. Edwin Wilmshurst

On the last day of steam on the Southern Region, Sunday, 9 July 1967, Salisbury-based rebuilt 'Battle of Britain' Light Pacific No 34052, the erstwhile *Lord Dowding*, is seen in steam on Weymouth shed with the former GWR coaling stage in the background. Credited with a lifetime mileage of 936,502 (428,516 as a rebuilt locomotive), No 34052 looks in fine fettle for a locomotive about to have its fire dropped for the last time.
A. Donaldson/Kidderminster Railway Museum 154464

On Tuesday, 27 June 1967, BR Standard '4MT' 2-6-0 No 76006 of Bournemouth shed stands in the shed yard at Weymouth with the former GWR 3-road straight shed in the background. The original northlight roof was replaced in 1930 by the one seen here. No 76006 went new to the Southern Region at Eastleigh in January 1953 and had four spells at Eastleigh, two at Bournemouth, and one at Dorchester and Salisbury before being taken out of traffic.
A. Donaldson/Kidderminster Railway Museum 154480

Nine Elms-allocated rebuilt 'West Country' Light Pacific No 34036, originally named *Westward Ho*, is seen here being turned on the manually-operated turntable at Weymouth shed on Tuesday, 13 June 1967. The 65ft diameter turntable is a typical GWR over-girder design and was installed in 1925. No 34036 was credited with a lifetime mileage of 894,546 of which 312,002 miles were run since August 1960 when it was rebuilt at Eastleigh Works. A. Donaldson/Kidderminster Railway Museum 154496

Weymouth engine shed was one of those chosen to collect together the Southern Region's withdrawn steam locomotives before disposal and cutting up. On Saturday, 5 August 1967 the yard holds a large number of former Southern and BR classes, both tender and tank engines, before they were sold primarily to the scrapyards of South Wales. A. Donaldson/Kidderminster Railway Museum 15447

0-6-0Ts, one 'E4' 0-6-2T, and all seven of the 'N15X' class 4-6-0s. By May 1959 this had been reduced to fourteen locomotives — one 'G6' tank, one '700' class 0-6-0, three 'N15s', three 'Schools' class 4-4-0s, two 'U' class Moguls, and four BR Standard '4MT' 4-6-0s.

The last locomotives allocated to Basingstoke shed were transferred away in March 1963, but the shed and its infrastructure were maintained until the end of steam to allow incoming locomotives to be serviced, and for locomen to sign on and off. The last steam locomotives allocated to the shed were 'Q' class 0-6-0 No 30541, 'U' class 2-6-0s Nos 31611, 31618, and 31806, and BR Standard '4MT' 4-6-0s Nos 75065, 75066, 75076, 75077, and 75079.

Weymouth

Unique among the Southern Region steam sheds that survived into 1967, Weymouth was a standard GWR straight-road shed that opened in 1885. It became part of the Southern Region in February 1958, losing its 82F shed code for 71G, before becoming 70G in September 1963. In March 1959 its allocation was still very much orientated towards Swindon, with '1366', '5700' and '8750' class 0-6-0PTs, '1400' class 0-4-2Ts, and '5100' and '4500' class 2-6-2Ts, '4300' class 2-6-0s and 'Hall' class 4-6-0s on the books, along with five BR Standard '5MT' 4-6-0s.

It was not until May 1961 that Southern locomotive classes began to be allocated when three 'N' class Moguls, Nos 31405-31407, arrived. In August 1963 the first of ten Ivatt '2MT' 2-6-2Ts arrived, and in August 1964 the first of eighteen 'Merchant Navy' Pacifics was transferred to the depot. The arrival of the

'Merchant Navy' Pacifics was a reflection of the inability of Nine Elms to maintain and service them adequately in its dilapidated sheds. The last former GWR locomotives at Weymouth were a handful of '8750' class 0-6-0PTs that remained until the end of the Summer 1963 timetable.

At the beginning of 1966 Weymouth's shed allocation stood at 23, comprising nine 'Merchant Navy' Pacifics, Nos 35007, 35012, 35014, 35017, 35022, 35026, 35028, 35029, and 35030, eight BR Standard '5MT' 4-6-0s, Nos 73002, 73016, 73018, 73020, 73080, 73083, 73113, and 73114, and three Ivatt '2MT' 2-6-2Ts, Nos 41284, 41298 and 41301. A year later, on 1 January 1967, withdrawals had reduced the allocation to fourteen — ten 'Merchant Navy' Pacifics, Nos 35003, 35007, 35008, 35012-14, 35023, 35026, 35028, and 35050 and four BR Standard '5MT' 4-6-0s, Nos 73002, 73018, 73020, and 73113.

In April 1967 electric services began running between Waterloo and Bournemouth further reducing the number of steam duties. As a result, the remaining 'Merchant Navy' Pacifics and BR 'Standard '5MT' 4-6-0s were moved respectively to Nine Elms and Guildford sheds. Weymouth shed, however, remained in use as a servicing, stabling and signing-on/off point. After the final weekend of steam operations on 8/9 July 1967 the shed was used as a collection point for withdrawn locomotives while they awaited disposal.

Guildford

The former L&SWR semi-roundhouse shed at Guildford dated from 1887 and was extended in 1896. Not being a true roundhouse, the shed required the services of a short-wheelbase tank

engine to shunt locomotives out of steam. In August 1950 the shed's allocation stood at 57 locomotives, with eleven 'M7' 0-4-4Ts, two 'L11' 4-4-0s, three 'G6' 0-6-0Ts, four 'T9' 4-4-0s, four '700' class 0-6-0s, four 'L12' 4-4-0s, seven '0395' class 0-6-0s, a dozen 'U' class Moguls, eight 'Q1' 0-6-0s, and a single 'E4' 0-6-2T, along with the shed pilot, 0-4-0ST No 30458 *Sir Ironside*. By May 1965 there were 28 locomotives based at the shed — nine 'N' and eight 'U' class Moguls, six 'Q1' 0-6-0s, four Ivatt '2MT' 2-6-2Ts, and shed pilot 'USA' 0-6-0T No 30072.

On New Year's Day 1966 Guildford shed was home to No 30072, 'N' class 2-6-0s Nos 31405, 31408, 31411, 31818, and 31873, along with 'U' class Moguls Nos 31639, 31791, and 31803. Also on the books at that time were BR Standard '5MT' 4-6-0s Nos 73022, 73029, 73037, 73043, 73065, 73081, 73082, 73087-89, 73092, 73093, and 73110 as well as '4MT' 2-6-4T No 80011. Exactly a year later the allocation had been reduced by ten to No 30072, BR '5MTs' Nos 73092, 73093, 73110, 73115, 73117 and 73118, BR '4MT' 2-6-0s Nos 76031, 76033, 76053, 76058 and 76069, and '3MT' 2-6-0 No 77014. At the beginning of the last week of steam, ten steam locomotives remained — Nos 30072, 73018, 73020, 73092, 73093, 73118, 73155, 76031, 76069, and 77014.

On my last visit to the shed on Sunday, 5 February 1967 there were ten locomotives on shed, Nos 30072, 34008, 34023, 34077, 73093, 76033/53/58, D2286, and D3047. Guildford shed's days of steam came to an end on 9 July 1967 when the last two locomotives, Nos 30072 and 34018, departed, No 30072 for a new career on the Keighley & Worth Valley Railway and No 34018 for scrapping.

The 'USA' 0-6-0T No 30072 is seen alongside Guildford shed on 9 July 1967 in company of BR Standard '3MT' 2-6-0 No 77014, just before the Mogul set off on its last journey to Salisbury. During its stay on the Southern Region, when allocated to Guildford between March 1966 and July 1967, BR Mogul No 77014 acquired a cult following, and was in great demand for rail tour duties. Keith Lawrence/Platform 14

The shed pilot at Guildford between February 1963 and July 1967 was 'USA' 0-6-0T No 30072, seen here shunting coal wagons in the days prior to the shed closing. The white handrails and buffers were applied when this tank engine was used to work a special two-coach train from Guildford to Redhill and back. No 30072 departed from Guildford for the last time on 9 July 1967 when it made its way to Salisbury for storage, before being sold to Richard Greenwood for use on the Keighley & Worth Valley Railway. Colour-Rail 307448

BR Standard '5MT' 4-6-0 No 73029 of Nine Elms shed works an up empty coaching-stock train past Guildford engine shed on 9 July 1967, where 'USA' 0-6-0T No 30072 sits on the turntable being prepared for its last run to the disposal sidings at Salisbury shed. Also on shed at the time was rebuilt 'West Country' Light Pacific No 34018. Keith Lawrence/Platform 14

A melancholy scene at Salisbury shed in July 1967 as three withdrawn BR '4MT' 2-6-4Ts keep company with a rebuilt Light Pacific, a BR Standard tender engine, and a 'USA' 0-6-0T. The disposal of the last Southern Region steam locomotives involved individual scrapyards tendering for a locomotive and, once sold, the engines were hauled dead to their final destinations. Colour-Rail 07448

Salisbury

The first engine shed at Salisbury was opened in 1847, but in 1901 the L&SWR rebuilt the depot as a ten-road straight shed. By 1922 the locomotive allocation stood at around sixty, a figure that increased in Southern Railway days. In British Railways days the shed roof was replaced. On 21 May 1949 the allocation then stood at 68 engines with five 'M7' 0-4-4Ts, six 'T9' 4-4-0s, three 'G6' 0-6-0Ts, five '700' class 0-6-0s, seven 'H15' 4-6-0s, one 'L12' 4-4-0, nine 'N15' 4-6-0s, five 'S15' 4-6-0s, one 'Z' class 0-8-0T, five 'U' and four 'N' class 2-6-0s, eleven Light Pacifics, and six 'Merchant Navy' Pacifics on the books.

By May 1959 Salisbury shed's locomotive allocation had been reduced to 47, with two 'M7' 0-4-4Ts, one 'G6' 0-6-0T, three 'T9' 4-4-0s, three '700' class 0-6-0s, two 'H15' 4-6-0s, six 'N15' 4-6-0s, eleven 'S15' 4-6-0s, one 'Z' class 0-8-0T, two 'N' class Moguls, eight Light

Pacifics, three 'Merchant Navy' Pacifics, and five BR Standard '4MT' 2-6-0s. On 1 January 1967 only a dozen locomotives remained, — Light Pacifics Nos 34006, 34013, 34015, 34052, 34056, 34057, 34089, 34100, and 34108 and BR '4MT' 2-6-0s Nos 76007, 76008 and 76067. Three of the Light Pacifics, Nos 34006, 34015, and 34057, were unrebuilt and still being used on standby duties covering any 'Warship' diesel-hydraulic failures on the Exeter and Waterloo expresses, despite Eastleigh having ceased giving the non-rebuilds general overhauls by the end of 1962. By this date Salisbury's Light Pacifics were invariably turned out in better external condition than any of the other extant sheds. The last week of steam saw Salisbury's allocation reduced to just five Light Pacifics, Nos 34013, 34052, 34089, 34100 and 34108. The last non-rebuilt Pacific at Salisbury, No 34057, had been withdrawn early in May 1967 with a cracked middle cylinder.

Eastleigh

Opened in 1903, Eastleigh depot was the major engine shed in the Southampton area and usually had an allocation of between 100 and 120 locomotives. With sub-sheds at Winchester City, Andover Junction, Lymington, and at Southampton Terminus and Southampton Docks, it was also responsible for the running-in turns from the nearby Eastleigh Works. In January 1947 its locomotive allocation stood at 126, and comprised six 0-4-0Ts, 22 0-4-4Ts, thirteen 0-6-0Ts, one 0-8-0T, ten 0-4-2s, eighteen 0-6-0s, 31 4-4-0s, seven Moguls, and eighteen 4-6-0s. By May 1949 this had fallen to 121 locomotives of which only No 34036 was a Light Pacific. Within a year this figure had risen to 142 and included eight 'Lord Nelsons' and eleven 'N15' class 4-6-0s. By May 1959 there were 111 locomotives allocated, these including thirteen of the fourteen 'Lord

Salisbury, like Weymouth, was chosen to hold withdrawn locomotives prior to their disposal to scrapyards, and in July 1967 'Merchant Navy' Pacifics Nos 35030 (minus its *Elder Dempster Line* nameplates) and 35013 (the one-time *Blue Funnel*) await their fate amongst a number of other steam locomotives. No 35030 was withdrawn from Nine Elms shed on 9 July and No 35013 from the same shed on 4 April 1967.
J. Tarrant collection/Kidderminster Railway Museum 150548

On an unrecorded date in 1967, BR Standard
'4MT' 2-6-0 No 76005 of Bournemouth shed is
being turned on the turntable at Eastleigh.
Coupled to a BR2 tender with a capacity of six
tons of coal and 3,500 gallons of water, many of
the Southern Region's '76000' class Moguls
were coupled to BR1B high-sided tenders with
a coal capacity of seven tons and a water
capacity of 4,725 gallons. No 76005 was
withdrawn later in the year, in July.
J. Fairman/Kidderminster Railway Museum 179944

On Sunday, 19 February 1967 Ivatt '2MT'
2-6-2T No 41319 and rebuilt 'West Country'
Light Pacific No 34018 (minus its *Axminster*
nameplates) are seen being serviced over the
ash pits at Eastleigh shed. At the time, the
Ivatt tank engine seen was allocated to
Eastleigh shed while No 34018 was on the
books at Nine Elms. Both locomotives would
see out steam on the Southern Region in July.
W. Potter/Kidderminster Railway Museum 006624

Pictured at Eastleigh shed on Sunday, 19 February 1967 is BR Standard '4MT' 2-6-0 No 76057 coupled to BR1B high-sided tender. The use of the
high-capacity tenders was a result of the Southern Railway, and its successor the Southern Region, not having any water troughs. The use of high-
capacity tenders can be traced back to the days of Drummond and his huge water-cart bogie tenders. No 76057 was one of Salisbury's dwindling
allocation of locomotives. W. Potter/Kidderminster Railway Museum 013933

In a commendable external condition, rebuilt 'West Country' Light Pacific No 34021, originally named *Dartmoor*, stands in the yard at Bournemouth shed on the penultimate Saturday of steam on the Southern Region, 1 July 1967, awaiting its next working. In the background is the shed's last steam pilot, Ivatt '2MT' 2-6-2T No 41224. Bournemouth shed was almost directly opposite the station, which made the comings and goings on and off shed easily accessible for interested observers. Barry Mounsey

Nelsons', the missing locomotive, No 30860 being transferred to Eastleigh shed in November 1959.

The first Light Pacifics allocated to Eastleigh, Nos 34004, 34016, 34022, and 34025, were not transferred until May 1961, yet by May 1965 the shed housed 23 'West Country' and thirteen 'Battle of Britain' Pacifics, 22 BR Standard '5MT' 4-6-0s, five '4MT' 4-6-0s, twenty '4MT' 2-6-0s, and twelve '4MT' 2-6-4Ts among its allocation of 103 locomotives. This dominance of Bulleid Pacifics and BR Standard classes would remain a feature of Eastleigh until the shed's demise.

On 1 January 1967 Eastleigh shed's allocation stood at 34 locomotives, with all but six of the locomotives either Bulleids or BR Standards. There were still five 'USA' 0-6-0Ts on the books, Nos 30064, 30067, 30069, 30071, and 30073, employed in and around the shed on pilot duties or in the docks at Southampton when required. The thirteen Light Pacifics on the books included non-rebuilds Nos 34023 and 34102, the latter destined to be the last in traffic. Also on the books were Ivatt '2MT' No 41319, BR Standard '5MTs' Nos 73119 and 73155, BR '4MTs' Nos 75068, 75063, 75064, 75076, 75077, 76061, 76063, 76064, and 76066, and BR 2-6-4Ts Nos 80016, 80139, 80151, and 80152.

During Eastleigh shed's last week of steam operations the number of active steam locomotives was down to 21. Remarkably there were still four active 'USA' 0-6-0Ts, Nos 30064, 30067, 30069, and 30071, along with seven Light Pacifics, Nos 34037, 34060, 34087, 34090, 34093, 34095, and 34102. Nine BR Standard locomotives were also still in traffic, Nos 75068, 75074-77, 76064, 76066, 80016, 80139, and 80152.

Bournemouth
The engine shed at Bournemouth was opened by the L&SWR in 1885 and was extensively rebuilt by the Southern Railway in 1936. In January 1947 its allocation stood at sixty locomotives, comprising three 0-4-0Ts, two 0-6-0Ts, nineteen 0-4-4Ts, four 0-6-0s, fifteen 4-4-0s, and seventeen 4-6-0s, but by May 1949 this figure had fallen to 55, but included five 'Lord Nelson' 4-6-0s, Nos 30861-65 and six 'Merchant Navy' Pacifics, Nos 35025-30. A rise to sixty engines in April 1959 saw the allocation divided between eleven classes — sixteen 'M7' 0-4-4Ts, two 'B4' 0-4-0Ts, one 'G6' 0-6-0T, three 'Q' and two '700' class 0-6-0s, seven 'N15' and three 'Lord Nelson' 4-6-0s, three 'U' class Moguls, thirteen 'West Country' Light Pacifics, and seven 'Merchant Navy' Pacifics. By mid-1965 the allocation had fallen to 39 engines with five 'West Country' and two 'Battle of Britain' Light

In June 1967, BR Standard '4MT' 2-6-4T No 80134 is seen on its home shed of Bournemouth being coaled by the depot's coal crane. Coaling practices at the Southern Region's last operating steam sheds varied from this use of cranes at Bournemouth and Guildford to the use of a cenotaph mechanical plant at Nine Elms, to the wheeled coal-carts employed at the former GWR engine shed at Weymouth. No 80134 would see out steam at Bournemouth before departing for Weymouth and disposal.
P.B. Whitehouse/Kidderminster Railway Museum 141689

Bournemouth shed on Saturday, 3 June 1967 is a hive of activity as an unidentified BR Standard '4MT' 2-6-0 raises steam alongside 'West Country' Light Pacific No 34023 which has had its *Blackmore Vale* nameplates removed for safe keeping. Behind No 34023 is the preserved 'A4' Pacific, No 4498 *Sir Nigel Gresley*, which is being serviced after working a special down from Waterloo. The LNER 'A4' Pacific would work another Waterloo to Bournemouth special on the following day. Colour-Rail 17630

BR Standard '3MT' 2-6-0 No 77014 stands on Bournemouth shed during the last weeks of steam on the Southern Region. Although the BR '3MT' Moguls were all built at Swindon and run-in on the Western Region, No 77014 was the only engine of the class allocated to the Southern Region between March 1966 and July 1967, after being transferred from Northwich shed. Colour-Rail 07448

Pacifics, nine 'Merchant Navy' Pacifics, eight Ivatt '2MT' 2-6-2Ts, eight BR Standard '4MT' 2-6-0s and seven BR '4MT' 2-6-4Ts.

At the dawn of 1967 Bournemouth engine shed was home to 21 steam locomotives, seven rebuilt Light Pacifics, Nos 34004, 34024, 34025, 34040, 34044, and 34047, five Ivatt '2MT' 2-6-2Ts, Nos 41224, 41230, 41295, 41312, and 41320, and BR Standard '4MTs' Nos 76005, 76006, 76009, 76011, 76026, 80011, 80019, 80032, 80134, and 80146. At the beginning of the last week of steam Bournemouth shed's locomotive allocation was down to fifteen, Nos 34004, 34024, 34025, 41224, 41320, 76005-07, 76009, 76011, 76026, 76067, 80011, 80134, and 80146. The shed's last pilot was No 41224, and during the last weekend of steam Bournemouth shed was cleared of steam with most of the locomotives being sent to Weymouth light-engine to await disposal.

Nine Elms
Opened during 1847/48, Nine Elms developed into the principal L&SWR engine shed. By 1926 it employed 820 men, of whom 468 were drivers and firemen. By August 1933 it had an allocation of 128 locomotives from seventeen classes. Most numerous were the 28 'M7' 0-4-4Ts, followed by eighteen 'N15' and seventeen 'H15' 4-6-0s, and ten Drummond

'T14' 4-6-0s. The remaining locomotive allocation comprised six 'S15' 4-6-0s, five 'Lord Nelsons', five 'K10', one 'T9', nine 'L11', three 'L12' and three 'S11' class 4-4-0s, two '700' class 0-6-0s, six 'G6' 0-6-0Ts, five 'O2' and three 'T1' class 0-4-4Ts, six 'U' class 2-6-0s, and the 0-6-0T shed pilot, No 756 *A. S. Harris*.

In January 1947 Nine Elms shed's allocation had fallen to 114 locomotives including ten 'Merchant Navy' Pacifics, Nos 21C11-21C20. Of the shed's 45 4-6-0s there were twelve 'N15s', eleven 'H15s', nine 'T14s', seven 'N15Xs', and six 'Lord Nelsons'. The twenty-one 0-4-4Ts were a mix of twelve 'M7s', three 'O2s', four 'H' class tank engines, and two 'R1s'. Of the seventeen 4-4-0s there were seven 'K10s', five 'L11s', three 'T9s', and two 'L12s' in addition to nine 'G6' 0-6-0Ts, two 'D1' 0-4-2Ts, five '700'class 0-6-0s, four 'U' class Moguls and 0-8-0T No 949 *Hecate*.

By mid-1959 Nine Elms shed was home to ninety locomotives — six ex-GWR '8750' 0-6-0PTs, nine 'M7s', three 'T9s', five 'N15s', nine 'H15s', three '700' class 0-6-0s, four 'Schools' class 4-4-0s, five 'U' class Moguls, five 'E4s', three 'Q1s', fifteen Light Pacifics, ten 'Merchant Navy' Pacifics, and thirteen BR Standard '5MT' locomotives. Within two or three years the run-down of steam on the Southern Region was gaining momentum, and by mid-1965 the shed's allocation was

down to 39 locomotives, made up of four Light Pacifics, nine BR Standard '5MTs', six '4MT' Moguls and 2-6-4Ts and fourteen '3MT' 2-6-2Ts. The beginning of 1966 saw the number reduced to just 24 locomotives and Nine Elms shed was displaying the years of neglect and the long-term effects of the wartime bombing of South London during the Blitz, and the onslaught of the 'V1' and 'V2' missiles.

Remarkably, on 1 January 1967 the locomotive allocation at Nine Elms had risen to 27, with nine Light Pacifics, two Ivatt '2MT' 2-6-2Ts, six BR Standard '5MTs', eight '4MT' 2-6-4Ts, and two '3MT' 2-6-2Ts still on the books. Then for the last week of steam workings the shed's allocation stood at 25, with five Light Pacifics, Nos 34001, 34018, 34021, 34023, and 34036, seven 'Merchant Navy' Pacifics, Nos 35003, 35007, 35008, 35013, 35023, 35028, and 35030, three Ivatt '2MT' 2-6-2Ts, Nos 41298, 41312, and 41319, four BR Standard '5MT' 4-6-0s Nos 73029, 73037, 73043, and 73065, four BR Standard '4MT' 2-6-4Ts, Nos 80015, 80133, 80140, and 80143, and two BR '3MT' 2-6-2Ts, Nos 82019 and 82019. On 9 July 1967 the last steam locomotive to drop its fire at Nine Elms shed was 'Merchant Navy' Pacific No 35030, which had worked up to Waterloo in charge of the 14.07 train from Weymouth.

In steam at Nine Elms shed amid the detritus of the soon to be closed depot on Thursday, 30 March 1967 is BR Standard '4MT' 4-6-0 No 75074 of Eastleigh shed, waiting time before picking up its booked down duty that will take it back to the Eastleigh or Southampton area. Behind, is rebuilt 'West Country' Light Pacific No 34108, originally named *Wincanton*, of Salisbury shed, which will be withdrawn in the June, while No 75074 would see out steam in July. Colour-Rail 10107a

By Saturday, 1 July 1967 Nine Elms shed was in a semi-derelict state, with just a handful of locomotives in steam and others stored awaiting disposal and scrapping. One locomotive being prepared for service was 'Merchant Navy' Pacific No 35003, once named *Royal Mail*, which was booked to work the 08.30 Waterloo to Weymouth boat train. Behind the Pacific can be seen the bunker of BR Standard '4MT' 2-6-4T No 80140 that was booked for station pilot and empty-stock duties. Barry Mounsey

Withdrawn unrebuilt 'West Country' Light Pacific No 34015 awaits disposal in the long shed at Nine Elms on Saturday, 1 July 1967. Allocated to Salisbury, the one-time *Exmouth* looks a little dusty, but otherwise is in reasonable external condition; only the dismantled motion is indicative that the Pacific will not steam again. Officially withdrawn on 16 April 1967, No 34015 would be sold to Cashmore's yard in Newport, South Wales, for cutting up. Barry Mounsey

The Southern Region's BR Standards

The Riddles-designed BR Standard locomotives were scattered far and wide throughout the British railway system, and **Jeremy English** *reviews the variety that were allocated to the Southern, some lasting until the end of steam on that region on 9 July 1967.*

The very first BR Standard locomotive to be allocated to the Southern Region was only the fourth one built, No 70004 *William Shakespeare,* and here we see this Pacific locomotive on 23 August 1954 leaving London's Victoria station at the head of the train for which it had been diverted from its planned allocation to the Great Eastern lines of the Eastern Region. The train is the 'Golden Arrow', which was one of a series of trains either introduced or re-equipped in 1951 and referred to as the 'Festival of Britain' trains as part of a major publicity campaign by the new British Railways. This engine had been exhibited at the festival and, sporting a special exhibition finish, had gone straight to Stewarts Lane shed to work the 'Golden Arrow', along with classmate No 70014 *Iron Duke.* R.L. Hyman

The BR 'Britannia' class Pacifics

The first BR Riddles Standard engines to be allocated to the Southern Region were three locomotives that the region really didn't need at all. With 140 Bulleid Pacifics (even if they didn't all work), three of the '7MT' BR 'Britannias' Pacifics were purely a BR publicity exercise in connection with the 'Golden Arrow' and, briefly, the 'Bournemouth Belle'. No 70009 *Alfred the Great* only stayed four months, working on the Western Division from 24 May to September 1951, the other more famous pair, Nos 70004 *William Shakespeare* and 70014 *Iron Duke,* remaining on the Eastern Division at Stewarts Lane until June 1958, having arrived in September and June 1951 respectively. Curiously, both were recorded working trains on the Western Division at times. Seven more 'Britannia' Pacifics, Nos 70017/23/24/28/29/30/34, were loaned to the Southern Region in May 1953 during the crisis when the Bulleid Pacifics had to be withdrawn for inspection following the driving-axle failure on 'Merchant Navy' Pacific No 35020 *Bibby Line* at Crewkerne.

One other Riddles-designed class of BR Standard Pacific locomotives which might have become Southern engines were the '6MT' class, as Nos 72010-14 were to have been built for the Southern Region during 1955/56 as part of the 1954 build programme but, probably as a result of the decision to

rebuild, rather than scrap, the Bulleid Pacifics, this order was cancelled. As a footnote, BR 'Britannia' Pacific No 70004 returned to the Southern Region briefly on 14 August 1966 on a rail tour, and then worked a few service trains on the Bournemouth main line.

The BR '5MT' class 4-6-0s

The first taste of BR Standard '5MT' power on the Southern Region came during the 1953 Bulleid crisis when Nos 73003, 73015, and 73017 spent a few weeks in May and June 1953 on the Southern Region. Having tackled its legacy of obsolete pre-Grouping tank engines and many (but not all) of its ancient 4-4-0s, the Southern Region turned to the 4-6-0s that it had inherited. However, the first allocation of BR Standard 4-6-0s, Nos 73050-52, were sent directly to the Somerset & Dorset line, and they all had 5,000gallon BR1A tenders. Although the S&D was not entirely 'Southern', motive power was the responsibility of the Southern Region, and its attempt to use Bulleid Pacifics on the line had been something of a failure. These three BR '5MT' engines remained on the S&D even through Western Region days from 1958 until 1964/65, the first of them then having an 'Indian Summer' on LMR lines until June 1968, the only steam engine to have worked from new for the Southern (of any type) to survive beyond 9 July 1967 in BR use, and then into preservation. No 73051 even got a coat of green paint (at Eastleigh in 1963) under Western Region rule.

Proper allocations to the Southern Region started with Nos 73080-89 in 1955. From June

until September these engines, built at Derby with BR1B 4,750gallon tenders, were delivered to Stewarts Lane to replace 'King Arthur' class 4-6-0s and 'Schools' class 4-4-0s on the Eastern Division, most of these Maunsell engines then transferring to the Western Division to replace the early Urie engines of the 'H15' and 'N15' classes. Then from October 1955, Doncaster-built Nos 73110-19, fitted with the largest BR Standard tenders (BR1F, holding 5,625 gallons of water), went straight to Nine Elms shed to replace more 'N15' class 4-6-0s.

The 73080-89 batch moved over to the Western Division as the sparks started to fly on the Eastern Division from May 1959, Nos 73085 and 73088 having spent a few months away at Oxford in February/March 1956, and No 73087 spending the summers of 1956 to 1961 at Bath (Green Park), joined by No 73088 in the summer of 1958, and No 73116 from the other batch during the period 1956 to 1959. Two more BR '5MT' 4-6-0s, Nos 73041 and 73042, joined the Southern Region ranks in June 1958 in exchange for the two Stewarts Lane BR 'Britannia' Pacifics. They also went to the Western Division in May 1959.

In September 1958, as a result of the transfer of Weymouth shed to the Southern from the Western Region, the latter exchanged Nos 73017/18/20/22/29 for five 'Halls' which the Southern didn't want. No 73018 had been painted green at Swindon just before this move; other BR '5MT' 4-6-0s which it had that were green at some time before transfer to the Southern included Nos 73029/37/92.

The first BR '5MT' 4-6-0s to be allocated to the Southern Region, in 1955, were Nos 73050-52. Fitted with BR1A tenders with inset bunkers they were sent to the Somerset & Dorset line to replace former LMS Stanier 'Black Fives', their design being a standardised version of the latter. Although no longer a Southern engine or at a Southern location, No 73051 is seen here at Templecombe on 13 May 1965 sporting the Western Region green livery, in which form it remained a familiar figure working to Bournemouth. Having spent its formative years on the Somerset & Dorset line it remained there under Western Region rule until the line's demise in March 1966. The engine in the background is, however, a true Southern one, being BR Standard '4MT' Mogul No 76014 of Eastleigh shed.

In April 1956, a year after its arrival on the Southern's Eastern Division, the first of the BR Standard '5MT' 4-6-0s allocated to the Southern Region, No 73080, is seen at Folkestone Junction waiting take over a boat train which would come up the steep climb from Folkestone (Harbour) station powered by 'R1' 0-4-4Ts. No 73080 sports a BR1C tender with a flush coal bunker in LMR style.   S. Creer

Fitted with the largest BR Standard type tender, BR1F, BR '5MT' 4-6-0 No 73116 leaves Southampton (Central) on 25 August 1956 with the 2.20pm Portsmouth to Bournemouth stopping train. The only other BR Standard class engines to have had these tenders from new were the '9F' 2-10-0s built for the Eastern and North Eastern Regions. The number 253 on the higher route disc shows that this locomotive is working Eastleigh shed's 253 duty roster.   L. Elsey

As a nod to those that they had 'killed off', Nos 73080-89 and 73110-19 inherited the names of Urie 'N15' class engines between 13 June 1959 and 3 June 1961 – a somewhat long-drawn-out affair! All remained in lined-out BR black livery. The nameplates started to disappear around the spring of 1965; some people unofficially called them 'Standard Arthurs'.

The BR Riddles '5MT' 4-6-0s seem to have been the most popular Standard type of all, being a simple development of the classic Stanier 'Black Fives' of the LMS. Although designated mixed traffic locomotives they did the lion's share of their Southern work on heavy main line passenger trains and fitted van work. All engines of the two Southern-only batches remained on the region until withdrawal, except No 73110 which had a two-month sojourn on the Western Region at Old Oak Common during February/March 1956. The first to go was No 73116 in November 1964, most of the rest departing during 1965/66, leaving six of the class, Nos 73085/110/113/115/118/119 working in 1967.

As with other BR Standard classes, a number of 'cast offs' from other regions made their way to the Southern in the mid-1960s. These were Nos 73002/16/43/46/65/155 from the Eastern Region in late 1962 and then Nos 73167-71, the last-built engines of the class, from the North Eastern Region a year later. By the beginning of 1964 nine engines of the class were at Feltham, used primarily on freight work, although No 73167 soon departed in August 1964 for Shrewsbury. The last to become 'Southerners' were Nos 73037 and 73092, which arrived at Eastleigh from the Western Region in April 1965. Out of all these engines the 'foreign' engines of the class, Nos 73018/20/29/37/43/65/92/155, remained working along with 'native' Nos 73085 and 73118 until the July 1967 last rites.

The BR '4MT' class 4-6-0s

Another BR Standard class of locomotives to be allocated to the Southern 'in bulk' from new was the '4MT' 4-6-0, eighty of which were built. This was a type that had no discernible pre-nationalisation origin so may be considered to be a new design to meet a Western Region requirement for a Standard locomotive to match its 'Manor' class, although they can also be described as a tender version of the BR '4MT' 2-6-4Ts, albeit with a different wheel arrangement. The Southern Region soon saw this design to be a suitable replacement for its Maunsell 'N' and 'U' class family to work the 'Withered Arm' lines west of Exeter, and the last order of fifteen locomotives, Nos 75065-79, was allocated to the Southern Region, arriving between August 1955 and January 1956; construction of Nos 75050-64 for the LMR was postponed to allow the Southern ones precedence. The first five went to Dover, and the final ten (from October 1955) to Exmouth Junction.

All the non-Southern engines of the class had BR2 tenders, but the Southern engines were provided with BR1B ones like the later BR '4MT' Moguls. This was because the Southern had no water troughs, and some of the engines were to be allocated to the West of England 'Withered Arm' services which involved quite long runs. Unfortunately nobody seems to have noticed that the bigger tenders had a 12-inch longer wheelbase, which made the overall wheelbase 51ft. Turntables at the various 'Withered Arm' termini were of the 50ft pattern, thus the engines were unable to be turned at the end of a run to Bude, Launceston, Barnstaple, and Wadebridge! The 70ft turntables had been installed at Padstow and Ilfracombe to accommodate Bulleid Pacifics. Thus there weren't enough duties for BR '4MT' 4-6-0s in the West Country and Nos 75070-02 were redeployed to the Somerset & Dorset line,

No 75074 to Eastleigh, and Nos 75075-79 to Basingstoke. Nos 75070 and 75073 swapped sheds nine months later.

The Somerset & Dorset BR '4MT' 4-6-0s replaced ancient ex-LMS '2P' 4-4-0s, but Eastleigh just used its pair alongside the contemporary '4MT' Moguls. Basingstoke used its engines to dispose of the former LB&SCR 'N15X' rebuilds and the last Urie 'N15s' on Waterloo stopping trains.

The BR '4MT' 4-6-0s, as introduced, were somewhat shy steamers and, like their forerunners, had to have modifications to bring them up to scratch. The Western Region set to improve them and declared that they needed double chimneys, the fitting of which started in 1957. Although the Western Region only converted nine of its twenty engines, the Southern was much more enthusiastic and converted all its engines, including the three Somerset & Dorset ones that it had gifted the Western Region back in 1958, between October 1960 and November 1961.

Before getting the new chimneys the Dover engines moved to Bournemouth in June 1959 upon the completion of the Kent Coast Phase One electrification scheme. Once again they were under-employed, and No 75069 went to the Central Division at Stewarts Lane to work Oxted line trains. There it joined Nos 75070/74/75 which had, at last, found a niche there earlier that year. Sadly it didn't last, and the engines became nomads, roaming around the Central Division until late 1963 when they ended up at Eastleigh or Nine Elms until withdrawn, No 75074 actually reaching the 9 July 1967 finishing line. In fact, Eastleigh became the final home for lost BR '4MT' 4-6-0s, all the remaining Southern engines (the three S&D ones had gone off with that line to the Western Region in 1958) ended their working days there, Nos 75068/75-77 also getting to the end of Southern Region steam.

One other locomotive at least was attached to a BR1F tender. BR '4MT' 4-6-0 No 75075 received one of the big tenders from one of the BR '5MT' 4-6-0s in its final days and is seen preparing to leave Waterloo with the 18.54 train to Basingstoke on 26 June 1967 as one of the 'Warship' class diesel-hydraulic locomotives, that had taken the West of England duties away from steam three years earlier, stands at an adjacent platform. J.H. Bird/Platform 14 K2534

The BR1B tender attached to BR Standard '4MT' 2-6-0 No 76053 almost overwhelms the sprightly Mogul as it heads for the Army exchange sidings at Ludgershall on the third line from Andover Junction towards the erstwhile Red Post Junction. The old Midland & South Western Junction Railway commenced at Red Post Junction, but this stub was all that remained by the date of this photograph, 13 May 1965.

The entire Southern allocation of BR '4MT' 4-6-0s was fitted with double chimneys in the late 1950s, and No 75077 is seen here double-heading one of the smaller '4MT' Moguls, No 76007, both Southern engines all their lives, when on the 09.15 engineers' train from Redbridge to Winchester, at St. Denys on 17 June 1967. Third rails abound on the main lines here, as the last parts of the system were being converted, these continuous welded rails being amongst the final ones to be installed. J.H. Bird/Platform 14 KO119

The BR '4MT' class 2-6-0s

To replace some of its elderly 4-4-0s such as the 'T9s', the Southern Region received its first batch of Riddles BR '4MT' Moguls, Nos 76005-19, from December 1952 until July 1953, all starting their working days at Eastleigh, but soon becoming spread around Western Division sheds. There they stayed until August 1956 when No 76014 went to Redhill for five months from August 1956 before returning 'home'. All remained on the Western Division until withdrawal, 2–6-0s Nos 76005/06/07/09/11 until the end of steam on the Southern, the others going during 1966/67, except Nos 76015 and 76017 the year before. Curiously, the first withdrawal, No 76017, survives today on the Mid-Hants Railway.

A second allocation of these Moguls, Nos 76025-29, arrived at Eastleigh in October 1953, these going for scrap a little earlier than their older siblings, from 1964 onwards, although No 76026 reached the end of steam on the region. These two groups would be supplemented by Eastern Region 'cast-offs' Nos 76030-34 in 1962 of which only No 76031 was a 'last gasp' engine in July 1967; these latter engines were built to the same order (for ten engines) as Nos 76025-29.

The former Eastern Region engines all had BR2 low-sided 3,500gallon tenders, but the remaining seventeen Southern engines, Nos 76053-69, became the only engines of the 115-strong class to be fitted with high-sided

4,725gallon BR1B tenders. Delivered between April and July 1955, Nos 76053-62 went to the Central Division at Redhill to work the cross-country line to Tonbridge and Reading, and the last seven were delivered in July and August 1956 to Eastleigh; these worked over most Western Division lines (Redhill giving up its allocation to Salisbury, Eastleigh, and Bournemouth during 1959/60) although only Nos 76064/66/77 survived to July 1967. The others went between October 1964 and June 1967.

The BR '3MT' class 2-6-0s

The 'oddity' on the Southern Region was the one-off allocation of a BR '3MT' Mogul, No 77014. This 2-6-0 locomotive arrived at Guildford in March 1966 to be used on a pair of excursions. Northwich, from whence it had come, didn't want it back, so it became allocated to Guildford for the rest of its life, becoming something of a pet, and outlasting all its siblings by way of surviving to the end of steam on the region, being used to head a parcels train from Bournemouth to Weymouth on 9 July 1967, the last steam-hauled train to arrive there.

The BR '4MT' class 2-6-4Ts

The first allocations of BR Standard engines was a batch of ten '4MT' 2-6-4Ts, Nos 80010-19, the first of the class to actually be built, having been both designed and built at Brighton (they were really a modified version

of the Fairburn tanks). From 10 July 1951 these tank engines went to Brighton and Tunbridge Wells West sheds to supplement the Fairburn tanks on the lines radiating from the latter as part of the policy to eradicate the remaining LB&SCR Atlantic and Pacific tanks. In February 1952 three more Brighton-built engines, Nos 80031-33, ordered for the North Eastern Region, never left Southern metals as three of the Fairburn tanks were sent north in their stead. Curiously, the remainder of this batch, Nos 80034-39, had been intended for the Southern Region but went to the London Midland Region.

Although Brighton kept building these BR '4MT' 2-6-4Ts tanks (it built all but 25 of the 155-strong class) it wasn't until it built the last ten, Nos 80145-154, in 1956 that the Southern Region received any more. These were really 'cast-offs', as the first five were intended for the Eastern Region and the last five were initially cancelled, but reinstated when it was realised that the boilers had already been

built! These engines joined their siblings on the Sussex lines, No 80154 going into service on 26 March 1957.

Logically, the Southern Region wanted to exchange all its remaining Fairburn tanks for BR '4MT' tanks, but none of the other regions wanted to do this, so it wasn't until Sunday, 29 November 1959 that any more went south. Then Nos 80034-43/59/64-68/81-85/87/88/89/94/95/137-144 came to the Southern from the London Midland Region, so as the 1960s dawned, the Southern had 57 of them. The newcomers were sent to work lines in Kent, then still being electrified. The first Western Division use saw Nos 80059/64-66/87/89/140 working from Bournemouth to Weymouth for a week from 2 October 1960 while Weymouth's turntable was being repaired.

The first allocations to the Western Division came in May 1962 when 2-6-4Ts Nos 80035/36/67 went to Exmouth Junction. In June, Nos 80037-43/59/64 joined them, whilst Nos 80065/66/82/83 went to Eastleigh,

with Nos 80087/95/137 joining the latter in the November.

The Southern then lost the remaining Exmouth ones! This was because the Western Region took over all Southern Region's lines and locomotives from 31 December 1962. Changes thereafter became frequent and widespread with, inter-alia, Nos 80087/95/137 going to Guildford in March 1963, Nos 80012 and 80148 going to Feltham in June, and Nos 80143 and 80154 going a month later. Nos 80081 and 80147 went to Weymouth, but soon on to Bournemouth, and the remaining Tunbridge Wells West engines went to Redhill (with a brief spell at Brighton) upon the closure of the former as a main shed in the September.

The year 1964 saw the first withdrawals, Nos 80010/87/148 in June and 80017 and 80031 by December. In the August, three were transferred from the Western Region, Nos 80069 and 80133 to Nine Elms and 80134 to work Bournemouth's duty over the

Although they might well have been ideal replacements for the ancient machines still eeking out an existence on the 'Withered Arm' lines in the 1950s, it was not until March 1966 that a BR '3MT' 2-6-0 was allocated to the Southern Region, for a rail tour. No 77014 stayed until the end of Southern steam, being used on various service trains such as the evening parcels train from Salisbury that is here seen arriving at Eastleigh on the final Friday of steam on the Southern, 7 July 1967. This Mogul would actually work the very last steam-hauled train of all on the Southern Region, the 20.30 vans train from Bournemouth to Weymouth two days later.
J. Fairman/Platform 14 JF0002

The penultimate BR '4MT' 2-6-4T, No 80153, was built at Brighton in 1956 and was allocated to the Central Division lines radiating from Tunbridge Wells. Here this locomotive is seen at Grove Junction, between Tunbridge Wells (Central) and Tunbridge Wells (West) stations, on 23 December 1961, heading the 12.10pm Tonbridge to Brighton train. This train would go via Uckfield and Lewes on the line which would later be severed between those two places. E. Wilmshurst

Somerset & Dorset line, this engine being in exceptionally poor condition. Four virtually useless members of the class, Nos 80070/96/102/132, were discarded by the London Midland to the Southern Region in April 1965; all but No 80096 went straight into store at Feltham, the latter going to Bournemouth, where it only lasted until the end of the year. The remaining engines on the Central Division were transferred to the Western Division in mid-June 1965, most going into store, and then withdrawal.

With just over a year to go in April 1966, a total of 28 remained; Bournemouth had seven members of the class, Eastleigh had seven, Feltham five, and Nine Elms nine. These soldiered on, losing a further twelve in the year so that just seventeen engines of the class reached 1967. At the end of steam on the region Nos 80011/15/16/85/133/134/139/140/143/146/152 dropped their fires, No 80146 probably being the last. Nos 80011/15/16/33/46/54 had spent their entire careers as Southern engines.

The BR '3MT' class 2-6-2Ts

The Southern Region actually had examples of all three types of BR Standard tanks. The middle-sized '3MT' 2-6-2Ts, which had been requested by and built by the Western Region as a Standard version of its Large Prairies, proved to be quite suitable for Southern duties as well. Nos 82010-19 went to Exmouth Junction when new from June to September 1952 and took over the heavier Exmouth branch duties and some 'Withered Arm' ones from 'M7' 0-4-4Ts. Nos 82022-25, intended for the North Eastern Region, also went new to Exmouth Junction during October and November 1954, replacing Nos 82012/14-16, which had moved to Eastleigh locomotive shed in early 1953 to be used primarily on the Fawley oil traffic.

Allocations remained pretty much static until November 1962, just prior to the Western Region take-over of lines beyond Wilton when Nos 82010-14/17-19 were transferred to Nine Elms to take over empty

One of the transfers from the London Midland Region during 1959/60 of BR Standard '4MT' 2-6-4Ts, in exchange for the Fairburn tanks that had been built at Brighton during 1950/51, is seen at Oxted station taking water. No 80144 is heading the 10.08am train from London (Victoria) to Tunbridge Wells (West) via East Grinstead on 26 January 1961, while 'H' class 0-4-4T No 31162 has coaching set No 663 ready in the opposite platform to form the 11.04am service to the same destination, but via Edenbridge.

After the demise of the 'M7' 0-4-4Ts in 1964, both BR Standard '4MT' and '3MT' tank engines were used for Waterloo empty coaching stock duties. Here we see '4MT' 2-6-4T No 80143 as it waits in the engine bay between the platforms at Waterloo on 14 August 1965 as its smaller sibling, a Western Region immigrant, BR Standard '3MT' 2-6-2T No 82006, awaits the right-away to leave the terminus after having brought in stock for a down working which had now departed.

On Saturday, 4 May 1964, the final day of services on the 'Old Road' through Ringwood, former North Eastern Region-allocated BR Standard '3MT' 2-6-2T No 82028 departs from Ringwood station with a down train from Brockenhurst to Bournemouth. The stock is a BR-converted Maunsell pull-push set operated as normal hauled stock since the BR locomotives were never equipped with the Southern's standard Westinghouse air-operated control apparatus. J. Read

The first of the Southern Region's BR '2MT' 2-6-2Ts, Darlington-built No 84020, is seen at New Romney station in July 1957 when just three months old. It was working the New Romney to Appleford branch services, having ousted the Wainwright 'H' 0-4-4Ts upon its arrival at Ashford shed on 23 March 1957. Although these engines were fitted with push-pull control apparatus this was the London Midland Region's version using vacuum, whereas the Southern's pull-push system used air pressure. Thus the economies of push-pull working, which had kept marginal services such as these at least as low-cost as possible, were no longer realized. Surprisingly, this line kept its passenger trains until March 1967, latterly worked by diesel units. R. Shenton/Colour-Rail BRS1323

Bottom: Although it was not until 1961 that any BR Standard '9F' 2-10-0s were allocated to the Southern Region (for the Fawley oil trains), they did visit the Southern Region from other BR regions on through or transfer workings. Feltham yard, on the Hownslow loop line in south-west London, was the Southern's principal marshalling yard for the Western Division, so BR '9F' No 92127 was taken there on 24 April 1957 to ensure that it could negotiate all of the tight curves and pointwork there. The turntable was a 70ft one, so the long engines would have no trouble being turned. Lens of Sutton Collection

coaching stock work from 'M7' 0-4-4Ts. Nos 82015 and 82016 followed a couple of months later, these engines remaining in the Metropolis until the end of steam on the region, when No 82019 worked the last 'Kenny Belle' on 7 July 1967. It had been the only one of the original Southern allocation to make it into 1967, but it shared this distinction with No 82029, one of a number of former Western Region engines which were transferred in sporadically in the last few steam years from other regions. This accounted for a few BR green-liveried examples of the class on the Southern as the Western Region had taken to applying this express passenger livery to almost anything since 1955. The engines involved in this mass immigration were Nos 82001/02/05/06/20/21/26/29/33/35/39/40/42/44.

The BR '2MT' class 2-6-2Ts

The Riddles-designed BR '2MT' 2-6-2Ts were virtually identical to the Ivatt LMS '2MT' tanks that were built at Brighton into BR days, and it is often overlooked that the Southern Region did actually have ten of the Riddles engines, Nos 84020-29, from March 1957 to September 1961, on its books. The BR '2MT' 2-6-2Ts spent most of their Southern time on the Eastern Division, although ex-Works examples from Eastleigh would often be seen working in the Southampton area for short periods.

There was a plan in 1960 to modify three of these 2-6-2Ts for Isle of Wight use, but it came to nothing as did a reconsideration of the plan in 1964, by which time the engines had been long-gone from the Southern. From June 1961 Nos 84024-27 worked out of

Brighton shed and Nos 84020-23 went to Exmouth Junction but were sent to London by May 1961.

The BR '9F' class 2-10-0s

In addition to BR '3MT' 2-6-0 No 77014 working on the Southern Region, other surprises were the five BR '9F' 2-10-0s that went to Eastleigh from the Western Region for two years to work the Fawley oil trains. The Western Region had really never wanted the '9F' 2-10-0s, so it eagerly gave the Southern Nos 92205/06/31 in January 1961 and Nos 92211 and 92239 in August 1961. These locomotives were made redundant in June 1963 and went to Feltham for three months before going off to York in that September as the Western Region most certainly did not want them back!

The Lymington branch
Britain's last steam-operated branch line

*The story of a Hampshire branch line, related by **Jeremy English**, that remained steam-operated for over one hundred years, becoming the last branch line in Britain to see scheduled steam-hauled trains.*

Former L&SWR Drummond 'M7' 0-4-4T No 30052 comes off the Lymington branch at Lymington Junction on 8 April 1964, a few weeks before the surviving engines of the class were withdrawn and steam pull-push operation on the Lymington line would cease forever. Shortly after, on 4 May 1964, all trains would cease to run over the line curving away to the right in the background; this was the original Southampton & Dorchester main line via Ringwood. This line had been downgraded when the line through the middle of the junction, the Bournemouth Direct line, via Sway, opened in 1888, the original line thereafter becoming known as 'The Old Road'. E. Wilmshurst

During the early part of April 1967 I took a day off work for some reason, so my mother took advantage of the situation and demanded that I went with her to Brockenhurst to view houses. We were ascending the stairs of one with which she was particularly taken in Sway Road when the whole place started to judder and rattle, especially the metal-framed windows. Looking out from one of them I saw, through the trees, a Hampshire diesel-electric-multiple-unit rolling along the main line on the opposite side of the road, and remembered that steam had ceased on the Lymington branch just a few days earlier. As a teenager I was a little out of touch with railways, my attention being on girls, beer, music, and cars at the time. Steam would soon cease altogether on the former L&SWR main line to Bournemouth as well, so this re-ignited my interest in railways and the last days of Southern steam.

Needless to say, despite my now liking the house, my mother decided against it and fell in love with the next one we looked at. This was at Setley, across whose plain trains on the Lymington branch had been steam-worked for nearly 109 years since the branch line's (unapproved) opening on 9 May 1858. It had taken Lymington Town Council twelve years to get from wanting a railway to actually

doing something about it as it initially merely associated itself with the Southampton & Dorchester Railway who had proposed to build a station at Latchmoor (on Sway Road, no less), but had been persuaded to relocate it on to the Lymington Road instead, resulting in traffic chaos at the level crossing, which persists to this day.

The Southampton & Dorchester Railway opened on 1 June 1848, and by the time a public meeting in Lymington was held during August 1853 the people of the town wanted their own branch line. Five years later it opened as far as Bridge Road (leading to a toll bridge over the Lymington river), a temporary wooden station being erected here as the permanent station was to be built on a swamp or mill pond that had to be drained first. This was indicative of Lymington's condition at the time as its days of glory, when it was a major ship-building port, were long past, due to the silting up of the river estuary; it had provided more warships in Tudor times than Portsmouth. Nevertheless, it was still important as the main ferry terminal for services to West Wight at Yarmouth, just four miles across the Solent, and yachting was becoming a major activity as the 19th century wore on.

The Lymington Railway was formally created by an Act of Parliament on 7 July 1856 and included provision for the company to purchase the toll bridge and the town quay with the ferry. The first sod was cut on

8 January 1857 so construction took barely a year and a half. It had little spare cash, and plans to celebrate its opening with a firework display and a balloon ascent had to be abandoned, much to the chagrin of *The Lymington Chronicle*.

There were few earthworks and few gradients on the four-mile route, and work involved the draining of the swamp. The first train, supposedly a private one, comprising an locomotive and one carriage, carried many members of the public who had rushed on to the train and taken over the carriage, so the directors and official guests had to ride on the footplate and tender! Official opening had to await a Board of Trade inspection by Colonel Yolland, which he performed three days later and approved the line, which he found to be 'in very good order'. However the L&SWR, who had absorbed the Southampton & Dorchester Railway and was to work all trains didn't accept this, and required additional sleepers in the track and strengthening of all underbridges before commencing services, delaying opening of the branch until 12 July 1858. The colonel had stipulated that, in the absence of a turntable at Lymington, the line should be operated on the 'one-engine-in-steam' principle, a situation that is still in use today, albeit, as we will see, after a period of full signalling and token working.

Curiously, in view of the original Act's provisions, the company had to go back to Parliament in 1859 to obtain powers to acquire

A view of the first terminus of the line that was on the west side of the Lymington River beside the level crossing, with the toll road and bridge for road traffic to the east bank (Bridge Road). Opened in July 1858, this temporary station was replaced fourteen months later by a permanent station at the foot of the modest hill up which Lymington High Street runs. This in turn became a through station and was renamed Lymington Town in 1884 as a result of the opening of an extension across the river over this bridge to a new Lymington Pier station.

the ferry across the river. In these early days passengers had to be rowed out to the ferryboat from the town quay, the ferryboats themselves working both to Yarmouth and Cowes. Around this time the L&SWR was in a rates battle with the LB&SCR over services to Portsmouth, and locals found it was cheaper to go to London via the ferry to Cowes then by another ferry to Portsmouth and then train to London! The fares war resulted in this aforementioned journey costing 3/6d rather than the Lymington Railway's fare of 13/- (both third class)!

Lymington's permanent station, on the site of the swamp, was completed and opened on 19 September 1860, and a new jetty was provided just beyond it, ready for use in July 1861. This would cause some friction with passengers as they often had to climb across merchant vessels to reach the ferry steamers, which was probably worse than being rowed out into the middle of the river as had been the case previously!

Since the early planning days there had been demands for an intermediate station on the line at Shirley Holmes, which was on the road to Sway and could thus provide for that village. From 10 October 1860 a platform was provided there, but without any station buildings; it was described as a station but was later to become known as a halt. Trains called there only during daylight hours and passengers had to wave for a train to pick them up, or notify the guard before departure from Brockenhurst if they wanted to alight, and the service was only applicable to or from Brockenhurst. It had been intended to move the old temporary station building at Lymington to Shirley Holmes as that had become redundant a few weeks earlier. That proved impractical and the building remained where it was as company housing until its demolition in September 1954. By then Shirley Holmes station was long gone, it becoming redundant itself in 1888 when the Sway cut-off line to Bournemouth was

opened, closing shortly thereafter. It was never shown in any public or working timetables and no tickets ever showed its name; passengers had to buy full-line tickets to Lymington or Brockenhurst.

The L&SWR, in the meantime, had taken over the Lymington Railway on 21 March 1879 and on 1 May 1884 it opened an extension of the line across the river from Lymington station (this becoming Lymington Town station) to a new pier on the opposite side of the river alongside deep water, increasing the railway's length to 4½ miles. A new station, Lymington Pier, was provided here and, at last, the ferryboats could tie up directly alongside the station. To allow more than one train on the line at a time some form of signalling was required, and after a period of 'Train Staff and Ticket working' full signalling, with new signal boxes at Town and Pier stations, was provided in 1889 in accordance with the provisions of the Regulation of Railways Act. The sections were from Lymington Junction (on the L&SWR's former Southampton & Dorchester main line at Latchmoor) to Lymington Town, and from there to Lymington Pier station. This

Former L&SWR 'M7' 0-4-4T No 60 (a number it bore through both L&SWR and Southern Railway ownership) leaves Lymington Town station to head across the river bridge to Lymington Pier on 9 July 1938 with the 3.06pm train from Brockenhurst. This train includes what is possibly a through coach, as the first carriage is a main line Maunsell Diagram 2001 corridor third coach rather than one of the ancient pull-push ones of the time. The two lines in the foreground led to the original jetty or landing stage from which Isle of Wight ferries sailed between 1861 and 1884, and to Lant's siding which was laid in here in 1935.
H.C. Casserley

remained the method of working until Monday, 10 April 1967.

The L&SWR trains were usually hauled by various examples of locomotives designed by the Beatties (father and son), including the famous well-tanks. both of the early 2-2-2WT variety, and the later 2-4-0WTs. Tender engines were also used, some Beattie 2-4-0s such as *Stromboli* (they had fabulous names!) which ended its days here. An attempt to link Milford-on-Sea and New Milton to Lymington Town station by steam road-buses in 1905 was a dismal failure and in the same decade old 'Ilfracombe Goods' engines appeared on the trains (the first one, No 282, had been run-in when new in 1872 on the line). By the beginning of World War I one of the slightly-younger 'Saddleback' 0-6-0STs of Beyer-Peacock 1875 origin was the usual branch-line power.

Ostensibly partly due to worries about security, in the event of war a plan to dig a tunnel under the Solent (where the navy ruled) in 1901 never got off the ground (or, rather, into the ground although test borings were started on the Keyhaven marshes). It is more likely that the L&SWR didn't want to forsake the ferry fares as the Solent crossing would become known as the most expensive sea crossing in the world in later days! Thus the Lymington branch entered the 20th century in much the same form as it would retain until the end of steam in 1967, although the signal box at Lymington Town station was re-sited next to Bridge Lane level crossing in the late 1920s.

Further development was primarily concentrated on the Pier station, a new slipway to enable cars to be loaded on to ferries being provided in 1938, this being accessed over a level crossing just short of the station platform. A short siding was also added here, and the station buildings were upgraded and a long canopy was provided. The original timber signal box opposite the platform was replaced by a modern brick-built flat-topped structure at the northern end of the loop in 1956, in which year the final station on the Lymington branch was built, a halt adjacent to the Wellworthy engineering business close to the A337 road, where it enters the town of Lymington.

As we have noted elsewhere in this publication, the end of steam on former L&SWR metals started during World War I when the first London suburban electrification was inaugurated on 25 October 1915. Its impact on the Lymington branch was soon felt, as the electric trains resulted in a cascade of locomotives and stock. The old Beattie-era locomotives were soon consigned to scrap, the early Adams Radial tanks (which never appear to have worked on the Lymington branch) were whittled down, and the three varieties of L&SWR 0-4-4Ts were rapidly redeployed to branch lines. Many of the smaller 'O2' class 0-4-4Ts would simply go straight across the Solent to take over the Isle of Wight services, whilst their larger brothers, the 'T1' class 0-4-4Ts, would start working the Lymington line as the war came to an end. These engines

were fitted with the L&SWR's wire-and-pulley system for use in pull-push operations, and this resulted in the Lymington trains being turned over to this mode of operation.

Two of Dugald Drummond's tiny railmotor-type tank engines of classes 'C14' and 'S14' had been tried back in 1907 without success, but the Adams engines so fitted were a total success. Both the L&SWR and, from 1923 after the Grouping, the Southern, invested heavily in pull-push systems, converting a great variety of stock for this purpose. The L&SWR had built some new ones in the flush of the Edwardian era of motor-trains and some of these gated stock sets saw a little use here. Both 'O2s' and 'T1s' thus monopolised the Lymington line in the post-war era until the beginning of the 1930s when Drummond's 'M7s' (the third largest of the L&SWR 0-4-4T design) took over.

Locomotives came from Northam (later Eastleigh) shed and, later on, Bournemouth as well, who became responsible for all duties in 1964. Some 'M7' class 0-4-4T workings took in services both around the 'Old Road' from Bournemouth (West) through Wimborne and Ringwood to Brockenhurst (the original pre-1888 Southampton & Dorchester main line) and the Lymington branch, so there was some variety in the individual locomotives seen. One 'M7' 0-4-4T was stabled overnight at Lymington in the small shed at the northern end of the station layout, and there seems to have been no consistency as to whether trains were pulled or pushed to Lymington.

As recorded elsewhere in this publication, World War II, and the failure of the Southern's post-war plans to replace the 'M7s' with Bulleid's 'Leaders', meant that the Drummond engines would soldier on well into nationalisation, even staving off the plethora of ex-LMS and BR Standard classes right up until 1964. The 46-year-old 'M7', No 30058, is seen here at Lymington Pier station on 3 September 1952 when the 1889-built signal box was still in position opposite the rather flimsy-looking station with its narrow wooden platform. The waiting and ladies' room was also quite narrow. H.C. Casserley

Prior to the introduction of the Southern's air-operated pull-push system in the early 1930s, other former L&SWR 0-4-4Ts equipped with the wire-and-pulley L&SWR system worked Lymington branch trains. In this scene an Adams 'T1' class 0-4-4T, No E8, is pictured at Lymington Pier station on 10 October 1928 with the 11.41am train for Brockenhurst. A set of old L&SWR wooden-bodied stock is seen being used. These tank engines were Adams's final tank engine design, built for London suburban work and, effectively, a larger version of his better-known 'O2' 0-4-4Ts that became the standard passenger type used on the Isle of Wight. H.C. Casserley

The L&SWR's wire system was not terribly satisfactory (although it lasted for over a quarter of a century) and the Southern Railway standardised on the LB&SCR's air-operated system from 1930 onwards. All the passenger push-pull stock was converted, but only the 'M7' tank engines, now rapidly becoming redundant in the suburban area, were fitted with the control equipment, so these engines took over all Lymington local workings thereafter. Five 'O2' class tanks were also push-pull-equipped, but only for use in the West Country; no 'T1' class tanks were done. Thus the local trains did not change in essence for 35-odd years, although the former L&SWR side-door push-pull sets slowly gave way, firstly to ex-corridor 'Ironclad' sets, and finally in 1960 to former main-line Maunsell corridor sets. A side-door push-pull-fitted loose coach was kept at Brockenhurst for strengthening purposes, and the push-pull sets were based at Bournemouth in a pool, which included services around the 'Old Road'. A number of CCT vans were also push-pull-fitted to work in with these sets.

Train services showed a gradual overall increase in numbers over the years after an early hiccup. At opening there were seven trains each-way on weekdays and three on Sundays. This proved to be over-ambitious and eight years on had been reduced to four down and five up trains daily, except on Sundays when none ran. Twenty years on, in 1886, there were seven down and six up trains, still weekdays-only. Nine up and down trains ran in 1892, two of which were mixed trains if required.

As the 20th century dawned there were ten trains each-way, whilst at the start of Southern Railway ownership there were sixteen down and fifteen up services in the summer, and by the 1930s Sunday services had resumed. Not all trains served Lymington Pier station. After some suspensions during the war, British

Railways, in its first year of existence in 1948, ran fourteen down and thirteen up trains in the winter timetable, and during the 1950s services returned to pre-war levels with through trains on Summer Saturdays which ran to and from Waterloo. There were a similar number of local trains during the week and on Sundays as before, varying only by one or two in number each year. This last pattern was retained until the end of steam in 1967.

Whilst in the last decade of the 19th century the line supported two daily goods return workings, freight traffic on the line was relatively thin and so no specific locomotives were allocated to Lymington freight work. For most of its existence a single goods train would be worked in conjunction with the Bournemouth to Brockenhurst pick-up services. This brought

The locomotive and stock for the first train of the day from Lymington to Brockenhurst was stabled overnight at Lymington. On 10 April 1955 'M7' 0-4-4T No 30058 illustrates how the coaching stock was accommodated without being detached from the locomotive. As can be seen, the siding beyond the engine shed was sufficiently long enough to hold three to four coaches, whilst the engine rested inside the shed. Here, the tank engine is seen having pulled forward to take water. E. Wilmshurst

Goods traffic on the Lymington branch saw a considerable variety of locomotives over the years. Despite the lack of turning facilities at the Lymington end, these were usually tender engines. Spanning the years we see Drummond '700' class 'Black Motor' 0-6-0 No 30695 of Bournemouth shed in the modest goods yard at Lymington Town station during the summer of 1949. The 'Black Motors' were effectively goods versions of the 'M7' 0-4-4Ts with which they had much in common, being the first of the Scotsman's designs for the L&SWR in 1896, and ordered by him on the strength of an outstanding order held in abeyance from the Adams era. He sought tenders from various locomotive builders without the Locomotive Committee's explicit approval, but that body accepted the tender from Dübs & Co of Glasgow, Drummond's home town! Thirty 'Black Motors' were built and arrived in early 1897, but as no more were added they never had a Nine Elms Works order number and were always classified by the running number of the first-built locomotive. They had just slightly shorter lives than their 'M7' cousins, the last one being withdrawn in January 1963. R.S. Carpenter Photos

small '700', 'Q' and 'Q1' class 0-6-0s, or Adams 'Jubilee' class 'A12' 0-4-2 goods or mixed-traffic locomotives to the branch. For much of its existence there were special schools trains for which a rake of corridor stock was allocated to the branch, working from Lymington Pier in the morning, and back in the afternoon. Brockenhurst had the local grammar school for the New Forest until it was converted to a sixth form college during 1969/70; there were also school trains on the main line and on the 'Old Road'. These trains also sported tender engines, these being restricted in size due to the 50ft turntable at Brockenhurst.

The short turntable also led to the use of smaller, or shorter, locomotives on the Summer Saturdays through services to and from London. These became quite celebrated in the early 1950s as the last haunt of the famous (in their day) Drummond 'D15' class 4-4-0s, and 'T9' class 4-4-0s also appeared at times. These were initially replaced by 'U1' class Moguls which were themselves superseded by the 'Schools' class 4-4-0s after they were ejected from Kent, and then Sussex, until their demise in 1962. BR Standard '4MT' engines then handled most of these trains until the end of steam on the branch.

Maunsell 'Q' and Bulleid 'Q1' class 0-6-0s usually worked these trains along the branch itself whilst the London engine was turned and serviced at Brockenhurst. The morning up London train started at Lymington Pier with the main-line engine already attached.

For the local branch services, Eastleigh performed small miracles to keep the 'M7' 0-4-4Ts going until May 1964, even cobbling together one locomotive from two on four occasions, but by then the youngest survivor, No 30480, was 53 years old and the oldest, No 30667, was apparently 67 years old. The latter was cheating, however, as it was one of the cobbled-together engines and its frames came from No 30128, which was only 53 years of age!

With the loss of the 'M7s' the Lymington branch also lost some of its magic' as BR Standard '4MT' 2-6-4Ts and Ivatt '2MT' 2-6-2Ts took over, although they were, at least, still steam locomotives. They carried on, with the Ivatt tanks staying overnight at Lymington and the BR 2-6-4Ts working during the daytime. This was because freight services over the line ceased from 9 August 1965,

meaning that there was no provision for coal, except back at Bournemouth, so rosters had to be designed to allow the engines to work back there daily.

The stock was usually still the 1959 BR Maunsell pull-push conversions, but no longer working in push-pull mode as the Ivatt 2-6-2Ts, although some were motor fitted (but not the Southern-allocated ones), had an incompatible LMS-derived system, and none of the BR 2-6-4Ts ever were push-pull fitted, thus running round at both Brockenhurst (involving shunts across both main line tracks) and Lymington Pier became the norm, and many photographs were taken of the engines at the end of the line seemingly inches away from taking a dip in the Lymington River, and so during 1967 the Lymington branch became widely known as 'BR's Last Steam Branch'.

The final date for the end of steam-hauled trains over the branch wasn't announced until a few days before it occurred on 2 April 1967, when Ivatt '2MT' 2-6-2Ts Nos 41312 and 41320 had charge of the last steam workings, the very last train being the 21.40 service from

Drummond's last locomotive design was to enjoy an 'Indian Summer' in the early 1950s on the Lymington through trains to and from Waterloo. The 'D15' 4-4-0s were the ultimate development of the standardised design which had given rise to the 'M7s', '700s', 'C8s', and 'K10s' which had been expanded to create the famous 'T9' 4-4-0ss (and 'L11s', 'S11s', and 'L12s'). All these classes were being decimated at the time, but three 'D15s' were kept for these summer-only trains in 1953 and 1954 due to the 50ft diameter of the turntable at Brockenhurst, and the wretched performance of the Maunsell 'U1' class 2-6-0s in 1952. Here we see 'D15' No 30464 at Vauxhall on Saturday, 19 June 1954 on the 1.28pm Lymington Pier to Waterloo train, this engine being withdrawn three months later at the end of the summer season. The 'U' class Moguls took over these trains in 1955. N. Sprinks

Maunsell's 'Q' class 0-6-0s were the preferred engines on the trains from Waterloo along the Lymington branch itself, taking over from the Waterloo engine at Brockenhurst. Damned by Bulleid as an obsolete design, they were simple and reliable, although they supplemented rather than replaced the 'Black Motors'. The 'Q' class 0-6-0 No 30549 is seen here running tender-first on to the branch at Lymington Junction on 1 September 1962 with the 8.49am train ex-Waterloo which it had taken over at Brockenhurst, the train probably having been worked by a 'Schools' class 4-4-0 from London. This unusual view shows the token exchange apparatus and platform at the foot of the signal box steps, and has glimpses of the Bournemouth main line just to the left of the tender. E. Wilmshurst

The junction station was always just Brockenhurst from its opening in 1847 until 1876 when the suffix 'Junction' was belatedly added, only to be dropped once again in 1888 when it actually became a double rather than a single junction with the opening of the Bournemouth Direct line. On 17 August 1957 push-pull-fitted 'M7' 0-4-4T No 30057, working with an Ironclad set strengthened by a former SE&CR 10-compartment third (the only Chatham electric stock ever built), is seen taking water at the west end of Brockenhurst's down platform which had been extended in 1936. The Southern had acquired sufficient land to join the Lymington branch directly to this loop platform by laying a third running line between here and Lymington Junction, but this was not actually done until October 1978, by British Railways! In the background can be seen the large marshalling yard installed here in 1943 as part of the D-Day preparations, but the turntable is just out of sight behind the second coach from the left of the rather mixed stock held here for the summer Saturdays New Milton to Swansea (High Street) through train. BR Standard '4MT' 4-6-0 No 75070 is seen running in light-engine on the up main line. H.F. Wheeller Collection, courtesy R.S. Carpenter

In the final years of steam on the Lymington branch almost any type of working steam locomotive could be seen on local goods duties, and here we see Maunsell 'N' class Mogul No 31873 shunting the yard at Lymington Town in July 1965, the goods service ceasing barely a month later, on 9 August 1965. There were just three sidings in the little yard, the two served by the turnout in the foreground here and the last part of the siding to the landing stage would all be removed by May 1966. The platform run-round, the engine shed siding, and the signaling, together with the goods shed siding, were all to be taken out of use on 3 April 1967 with the end of steam working on the line. On the same day the level crossing was converted to full lifting barriers controlled by CCTV cameras from Brockenhurst, and the line became just a siding from the junction at Latchmoor. The sidings themselves were all lifted by April 1968. J.H. Bird/Platform 14 C3530

Lymington Town station saw very little in the way of alterations, other than to its small train shed that must have been quite some comfort to passengers for over a hundred years. Evidently, British Railways thought passengers would be quite happy to wait for trains without shelter and so closed the waiting rooms in the building and removed the train shed. On 25 June 1966 BR Standard '4MT' 2-6-4T No 80019 is seen working bunker-first to Lymington Pier station with the somewhat unusual short-armed down starter signal off for it to proceed over the river. E. Wilmshurst

Lymington Pier, where BR '4MT' 2-6-4T No 80019 is seen at the end of the line running round its train, as had become necessary for every train following the cessation of push-pull working some two years earlier. In the background is the Lymington River estuary, a new ferry terminal being provided here in 1976, and a new platform being built on the eastern side of the track. E. Wilmshurst

Lymington Town headed by the former engine, whilst the latter locomotive headed an enthusiasts' excursion earlier in the day. Although we lose all interest in the line after that, it may be as well to complete the circle by noting that the following day, Hampshire diesel-electric-multiple-unit No 1103 took over all duties, but this was only a short-term solution as the branch was electrified, and electric units worked passenger trains over the line from 1 June 1967, which is still the case today.

On Sunday, 26 March 1967 as the end of steam on the Lymington branch draws nearer, Ivatt '2MT' 2-6-2T No 41224 comes off the Lymington branch and past Lymington Junction signal box with the two-coach 11.28 Lymington Pier to Brockenhurst train. Note the red-backed 'Last Steam Branch' plate on the smokebox door of the tank engine, a board that Lymington branch trains carried during those final days of steam over the branch. The main line to Bournemouth is seen heading away in the distance. Colour-Rail

The pastime of visiting workshops, engine sheds and perhaps the oddities and outposts of the railway network soon became, as the 1950s rolled on, a mechanism for recording and commemorating notable dates, and all too often forming the last rites of redundant railway routes as they passed into history.

Locomotives and working arrangements changed in this era too, with railtour operators frequently requesting engines that were on their way out, as more modern locomotives, including a fleet of standard steam engines and those displaced by the continuing spread of electrification, became available, and latterly the diesel and electric products of the 1955 modernisation plan further changed the scene. The Southern Region had also taken in two notable Colonel Stephens railways - the East Kent, and Kent & East Sussex which had existed outside of the Southern Railway after the Grouping.

Amongst the most prolific rail tour operators on the Southern in this era were the Locomotive Club of Great Britain (LCGB), Rail Enthusiast Club (REC), Railway Correspondence & Travel Society (RCTS), and the Stephenson Locomotive Society (SLS).

Over the years, many rail tours have been run as an opportunity to traverse freight-only lines, or to mark the end of a class or closure of a line. On 3 May 1953 ex-L&SWR 'M7' 0-4-4T No 30110, with push-pull sets Nos 36 and 31, was employed by the Stephenson Locomotive Society on a charter to mark the closure of the Gosport to Fareham line to passengers, but was billed as the 'Bishop's Waltham Special' as it ran from Gosport to Bishop's Waltham, a branch terminus which had closed to passengers back in 1933. Here the train is seen exiting Fareham tunnel No 2 at Funtley, and nears Fareham on its return from Bishop's Waltham. Tour participants had arrived from London (Victoria) via Dorking behind 'Brighton' Atlantic No 32425, then had taken a ferry from Portsmouth across the harbour to Gosport to join the tour. This was ironic, as it was the very convenience of this ferry and the fast electric services at Portsmouth that killed off the Gosport line passenger service! Return to Waterloo later was behind former L&SWR 'T9' 4-4-0 No 30718 via Petersfield. L. Elsey

Former LB&SCR 'D3' 0-4-4T No 32390 is pictured on rail tour duties for the RCTS in the down Keymer line platform at Lewes on Sunday, 4 October 1953. Most 'D3' class 0-4-4Ts were push-pull fitted, but the class was nearly extinct by this time, although this engine did linger on until September 1955 on Oxted services. The tour started and finished at Three Bridges, taking in East Grinstead, the Cuckoo line, Polegate, the goods lines around Lewes, and the Bluebell line. The Southern would have eliminated much of the inherited steam fleet and be well advanced with electrification if World War II and railway nationalisation had not intervened. As a result, many locomotives including the 'D3s' survived much longer than envisaged, and BR soon found itself with a dilemma with how to keep push-pull services operating. The solution was to transfer the apparatus off the withdrawn engines on to former SECR 'H' class 0-4-4Ts which were not push-pull fitted until the BR era, and then nearly all had the apparatus fitted in the end. N. Sprinks

The ex-LB&SCR 4-4-2 Atlantic, No 32424 *Beachy Head,* has just passed through Wivelsfield station and nears Keymer Junction with the RCTS 'Sussex Coast Express' rail tour from London (Victoria) on Sunday, 13 April 1958. The tour was billed as the final duty for this Atlantic locomotive and at Keymer Junction it forked east to head for Newhaven Harbour; presumably the destination was deemed close enough to tip a hat to the real Beachy Head, just along the coast! A shuffle with Terrier tank No 32460 at Newhaven was followed by the use of the last locomotive to be built at Brighton as it hauled the tour to Brighton. A 'King Arthur' 4-6-0, No 30796 *Sir Dodinas le Savage,* returned the tour back to London in the evening. The stock is of interest as it is essentially a boat train set including Maunsell nondescript brakes at each end and, with Pullman car *Myrtle* centre stage. E. Wilmshurst

Ex-L&SWR 'M7' class 0-4-4T No 30107 pauses at Dorchester (West) on its return from West Bay and the Bridport branch when on an REC rail tour on Saturday, 7 June 1958. The sight of an 'M7' here on a former Great Western line was no doubt still regarded as a novelty at the time, but in fact all lines south of Castle Cary had come under the Southern Region in 1950, encompassing all the former GWR lines in Dorset. The paradox of regional boundaries in the BR era often saw no change on the ground, with an arbitery line on a map being irrelevant to the operating departments, even though it looked neat to the accountants on a map. Eventually however, change was apparent, and in 1957 BR closed the Southern shed at Dorchester, with operations moved to the Great Western shed at Weymouth, then over the next few years the pattern of passenger services moved away from Paddington thinking towards Waterloo. Colour-Rail BRS971

Former SER 'O1' class 0-6-0 No 31258 has recessed in the sidings at Deal on Saturday, 23 May 1959 during an REC tour of minor lines and sidings around the Kent coalfield. Three members of the class were still in traffic, with Nos 31048, 31065, and 31258 retained at Dover, ostensibly to work the lightly-laid remaining 3-mile section of the former East Kent Railway between Shepherds Well and Tilmanstone colliery. The tour started after lunch at Shepherds Well and visited Tilmanstone and Betteshanger collieries, Richborough sidings, and terminating at Kearsley up bay at 4.56pm. The 4-wheeled van was included in the formation for bicycles. Colour-Rail BRS1143

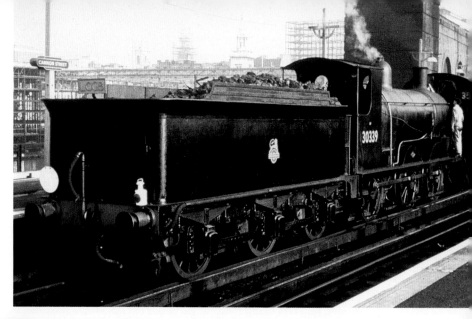

A former L&SWR '700' class 0-6-0, No 30339, awaits departure from London's Cannon Street station with 'The South Western Limited' LCGB rail tour on 18 September 1960. This was former SE&CR territory, and well away from home turf for an engine of this class but, after a reversal at Ludgate Hill, the South Western line was reached at Clapham Junction *en route* to an engine change at Ascot. The '700' class 0-6-0s were gradually being displaced by Crompton 'Type 3' diesels, with the remaining examples officially withdrawn in December 1962, but a number were soon re-activated for snow-clearing duties into 1963. However, although no longer in service, there was no hurry to move on the examples at Exmouth Junction, and two of the three there ended up moving to Eastleigh Works for disposal under their own steam in December 1963 and January 1964, over a year after they were struck off the books. Colour-Rail BRS1099

Above: **BR Standard '4MT' 4-6-0 No 75070 gets underway from Southampton (Terminus) with the RCTS 'Solent Rail Tour' at Chapel Crossing on Sunday, 20 March 1966.** Changed work patterns and line closures had reduced the use of Southampton's Terminus station and only hourly diesel-electric-multiple-units to Reading (General) and to Alton remained, with the threat of closure looming large; all were eventually withdrawn from 5 September 1966. This rail tour had left Waterloo behind 'Battle of Britain' Light Pacific No 34089 *602 Squadron* and due to electrification work on the main line was routed to Salisbury where 4-6-0 No 75070 was ready to take over for a visit to the Ocean Terminal in the Old Docks at Southampton. Two 'USA' 0-6-0Ts, Nos 30073 and 30064, were employed on an outing to Fawley over a branch line that had closed to passengers the previous month. No 75070 relieved the tour again at Southampton (Terminus) station for the short hop to Fareham where one of the last Maunsell 'U' class Moguls, No 31639, worked the trip to Gosport and back. The two locomotives were paired up and returned to London via the Portsmouth Direct line and Oxshott. P.J. Russell

Left centre: **The Maunsell 'Schools' class 4-4-0 No 30925 *Cheltenham*, with BR Mk I coaching set No 279, nears Merstham with the first leg of the RCTS 'Sussex Special' rail tour from London Bridge to Brighton on Sunday, 7 October 1962.** There were still twenty of the original forty engines of the class on the books at the time, with most at work on the Western Section. The tour also featured former LB&SCR 'E6' class 0-6-2T No 32418, 'AIX' Terrier tank No 32636, and returned to London behind 'K' class Mogul No 32353. It is not difficult to see why these locomotives were selected for this tour as all of these classes, except for the Terriers, were to be victims of the accountants' pen, being withdrawn before the end of the year. The Terrier tanks had survived this late, principally due their use on Hayling Island branch and K&ESR duties, and the stay of execution into 1963 was only pending closure of the lines that had ensured their survival this far! The overgrown and disused line to Greystone lime works is seen in the foreground. R.C. Riley

Left: **In the late evening of Sunday, 13 June 1965, the LCGB's 'Wealdsman' rail tour, with SR 'Q1' 0-6-0s Nos 33027 and 33006, has paused at Baynards for a prolonged 14-minute photographic stop.** The extensive tour included two lines that were scheduled to close from the following day, the Cuckoo line between Redgate Mill Junction and Heathfield, and this line, the former LB&SCR line between Christ's Hospital and Peasmarsh Junction via Cranleigh. With no Sunday service, the last public service trains had run the previous day, and so this tour would form the last passenger train over the route. Driver Jock Myles and fireman Bill Moore on No 33027, and driver Doug Stent and fireman Dave Newbury on No 33006, had earlier run over light-engine from Guildford with the pair of 'Charlies' to relieve 'Battle of Britain' Light Pacific No 34050 *Royal Observer Corps* at Horsham. E. Wilmshurst

The penultimate weekend of Southern steam

Barry Mounsey, *with help from* **Stephen Howarth**, *recalls some of the last days of Southern Region steam. All photographs by Barry Mounsey.*

A 'Merchant Navy' class Pacific, No 35003, minus its *Royal Mail* nameplates, simmers in Nine Elms yard on the penultimate Saturday of steam working on the Southern Region, Saturday, 1 July 1967. By this date all the 'Merchant Navy' Pacifics still in use that had been allocated to Weymouth shed had all been moved back to Nine Elms. No 35003 was the only Pacific locomotive in full steam at the time of my early morning visit to the shed and would go on to see further use during the following week.

A small group of us in the Jubilee Railway Society decided to travel south from Yorkshire for the penultimate weekend of steam on the Southern Region — Friday, 30 June to Monday, 3 July 1967. We knew we were leaving it late in the day and it would be a gamble as to how much steam we would find. Fifty years ago there was no up-to-date information available to enthusiasts as *The Railway Magazine, Modern Railways, Railway World,* and *The Railway Observer* were always one to two months behind real-time activity.

With the die cast, we all met up at Leeds (City) station on Friday, 30 June to catch the 22.15 overnight train to St. Pancras with 'Peak' class diesel No D76 in charge. Waking up at Sheffield and Derby to see any steam activity we tried to sleep as best we could for the rest of the journey. Arriving bleary-eyed in London in the early hours of Saturday we made our way south of the River Thames to Nine Elms shed. There was little in the way of steam on shed,

apart from 'Merchant Navy' class Pacific No 35003 *Royal Mail* being prepared for a down working along with BR Standard '5MT' 4-6-0 No 73093. Also in steam were a couple of tank engines — an Ivatt '2MT' 2-6-2T and BR Standard '4MT' 2-6-4T No 80145 booked for station pilot and empty coaching-stock turns in and out of Waterloo. Inside the shed in light steam was 'West Country' Light Pacific No 34024 *Tamar Valley.*

Although not officially withdrawn until 9 July 1967, 'West Country' class Light Pacific No 34100 sits, out of steam, inside the 'New' shed at Nine Elms on 1 July. The 'Not To Be Moved' sign on the front lamp-bracket suggests that the one-time *Appledore* has been laid aside, although all the motion is still in place. The tidy appearance of the paintwork shows that No 34100 is a Salisbury allocated engine, the one shed that made a real effort to turn out its Pacifics in a presentable condition throughout 1967.

One of Nine Elms shed's two remaining BR Standard '3MT' 2-6-2Ts, No 82019, is seen on station pilot duties at Waterloo on Saturday, 1 July 1967. Pictured at the head of a rake of empty carriages it will soon take these out to the sidings at Clapham Junction for servicing before working back to the terminus with the empty stock for a down working. On the evening of Friday, 7 July 1967 No 82019 worked the last steam-hauled unadvertised passenger working from Kensington Olympia to Clapham Junction.

Apart from *Tamar Valley* the straight shed was a depressing sight with rows of dead Bulleid Pacifics. By now the sun was shining through the roof, lifting the gloom somewhat, but with so little steam in and around the shed our weekend prospects looked very bleak, so we turned our backs on Nine Elms shed and made our way to Waterloo station where our luck was in as 'Merchant Navy' Pacific No 35030 *Elder Dempster Line*, in reasonably clean condition, was waiting its departure time. Presenting our tickets at the platform gates we were told that our 'Rover Tickets' were not valid on this train, which was an unusual special for House of Commons members for a return trip to Bournemouth.

After waiting some time, 'Merchant Navy' Pacific No 35003 *Royal Mail* backed on to

The last of the British Railways-built batch of 'Merchant Navy' Pacifics, No 35030, running without its *Elder Dempster Lines* nameplates, pulls out of Waterloo in charge of the return House of Commons special to Bournemouth. No 35030 has been cleaned for the occasion, while the welded patches on the tender show where leaks have been staunched. No 35030 would be in traffic nearly every day during the last week of steam, culminating in being the final 'Merchant Navy' Pacific in action on the last Sunday when it worked the Sunday-only 02.30 Waterloo to Poole service, returning with the 14.07 train ex-Weymouth.

Although out of steam at Weymouth on Saturday, 1 July 1967, BR Standard '5MT' 4-6-0 No 73093, officially still on the books of Guildford shed, would be lit-up on the Sunday for its final week in traffic. Among its final workings were the 07.18 Waterloo to Salisbury and the 15.55 Salisbury to Basingstoke trains. Weymouth shed, by this date, had been relegated to the status of a servicing and signing-on point having lost its last steam allocation at the end of April when its 'Merchant Navy' Pacifics were transferred to Nine Elms shed and its BR Standard locomotives to Guildford.

Two special trains were organised for Sunday 2 July 1967 and the beautifully turned-out 'Merchant Navy' Pacific No 35008 *Orient Line* heads for Bournemouth and Weymouth as it passes through Pokesdown station in charge of the 'Farewell to Southern Steam No 1' special. For the return trip to Waterloo No 35008 was piloted by classmate No 35007 as far as Bournemouth, with the two Pacifics turning in a spectacular performance. No 35007 came off at Bournemouth leaving *Orient Line* to take the train back to London.

another set of coaches. Again we were not allowed to board the train as it was the 08.30 boat train for Weymouth that was not covered by our tickets, and should have been worked by a Brush 'Type 4' diesel locomotive. Rather than be stranded at Waterloo all day we decided to cut our losses and catch an electric-multiple-unit to Bournemouth and book into our bed & breakfast hotel overlooking the engine shed.

While still on the platform at Bournemouth our luck changed on hearing the sound of steam arriving from the north-east in the form of BR Standard '5MT' class 4-6-0 No 73093, in charge of the 12.35 Waterloo to Weymouth train, a locomotive that we had seen at Nine Elms earlier in the day. We boarded this train and were soon speeding our way to Weymouth. In better spirits and with the sun out we would, of course, had preferred a Bulleid Pacific but you can't have everything. We were soon pulling

into Weymouth and a brisk walk found us wandering round the engine shed that no longer had its own allocation of steam locomotives. We found row after row of withdrawn locomotives, predominantly Bulleid Pacifics and BR Standard types, but also enough that were obviously still in use, but out of steam over the weekend.

What we didn't know was that we missed a Waterloo to Southampton Docks boat train worked by nothing bigger than a BR Standard '4MT' class 2-6-0, No 76064. Then while on the train to Bournemouth we also failed to see Southern Light Pacific No 34025 *Whimple* on the 09.24 Bournemouth to Waterloo service.

After making a note of all we saw, the sound of a steam locomotive working hard drew us to the lineside in time to see another Light Pacific, No 34018 *Axminster,* in charge of the Channel Islands boat train heading for Waterloo. It was then time to return to Bournemouth behind a Crompton 'Type 3'

Bo-Bo diesel (Class 33)-powered push-pull working, to book in at our bed and breakfast accommodation, and to ponder what our plan of action should be for the next day.

Sunday morning turned out sunny, so Stephen and I changed plans to spend Sunday night sleeping rough while the rest of the group headed back north. We made our way to Pokesdown station behind Crompton 'Type 3' diesel No D6521 to photograph two specials hauled by 'Merchant Navy' Pacific No 35008 *Orient Line* and classmate No 35028 *Clan Line,* and we were nearly caught by surprise as Light Pacific No 34025 *Whimple* rolled in with the Sunday-only 09.33 Waterloo to Bournemouth train. No 35008 *Orient Line* appeared, looking immaculate and complete with nameplates, but no smokebox number plate, and so we then retraced our steps to Bournemouth to see *Clan Line*, complete with name and number plates, arrive with the second of the specials.

Left: **The 'Farewell to Southern Steam No 2' special also ran on Sunday, 2 July 1967 as the 12.20 return trip from Waterloo to Bournemouth and was worked by 'Merchant Navy' Pacific No 35028** *Clan Line.* **The 4-6-2 locomotive was turned out in immaculate condition, complete with nameplates and smokebox number plate. Upon withdrawal from Nine Elms shed on 9 July** *Clan Line* **immediately passed into the ownership of the Merchant Navy Preservation Society.**

Right: **Although given its last light casual repair at Eastleigh Works in February 1966 'West Country' Light Pacific No 34025, originally named** *Whimple*, **was one of the most active of the Light Pacifics in the last days of Southern steam. In the fading light of Sunday, 2 July 1967 it waits to leave Woking in charge of the 19.59 Bournemouth to Waterloo train. It is recorded to have worked on each of the next five days before being set aside for scrapping.**

Rebuilt 'West Country' Light Pacific No 34037, running without its *Clovelly* nameplates, waits to leave Winchester on Sunday, 2 July with the Sunday-only 19.36 Bournemouth to Waterloo service. No 34037 was allocated to Eastleigh from June 1966 until withdrawn on 9 July, and thanks to a light casual repair at Eastleigh Works in June 1966 was able to work through to the end of steam on the Southern Region without needing anything other than routine maintenance.

We killed time by visiting Bournemouth shed again before sneaking on to the return special behind *Orient Line* as far as Southampton. An electric-multiple-unit took us to Eastleigh where we saw *Clan Line* heading for Waterloo. Then it was back to Bournemouth to catch the 19.36 service to Waterloo as far as Winchester behind Light Pacific No 34037 *Clovelly*. Here we waited for *Whimple* on the returning Sunday-only train that took us to Woking where we planned to spend the night.

After nodding off, we were brought back to consciousness by the sound of approaching steam in the shape of Light Pacific No 34013 *Okehampton* in charge of the 02.30 Waterloo to Portsmouth parcels train. The prospect of more steam mileage and a comfortable seat to Basingstoke proved irresistible but, before we

departed, No 34037 *Clovelly* arrived in charge of the 02.45 Waterloo to Portsmouth train.

Basingstoke allowed some more sleep before we were roused by the sounds of BR Standard '4MT' class 4-6-0 No 75040 at the head of the 04.40 Waterloo to Woking train which then became the 06.30 Woking to Salisbury service. Stephen left me here to travel behind No 75040, and it was not long before a grimy Light Pacific, No 34060 *25 Squadron,* appeared with the 06.49

Salisbury to Waterloo service. This was shortly followed by the 07.18 Waterloo to Salisbury train in the charge of BR Standard '5MT' 4-6-0 No 73093. The next steam working brought No 34025 *Whimple* in with the 06.22 Bournemouth to Waterloo train. Even freight was still in the hands of steam as BR Standard '5MT' 4-6-0 No 73029 passed Basingstoke complete with hand-made front number plate made by Eastleigh fitter Ron Cover.

BR Standard '5MT' 4-6-0 No 73093, one of ten engines of the class active during the last week of steam on the Southern Region, stands at Basingstoke after taking water when in charge of the 07.18 Waterloo to Salisbury train on Monday, 3 July 1967 and is now waiting for the signals to clear. Hidden under the layers of grime is the lined passenger green livery that was first applied at Wolverhampton (Stafford Road) Works in May 1960. No 73093 was allocated to Guildford shed at the time, having previously been on the books of Eastleigh shed between April and October 1965.

A 'West Country' Light Pacific, No 34025, running without its *Whimple* nameplates, makes a dramatic departure from Basingstoke when in charge of the 06.22 Bournemouth to Waterloo train on Monday, 3 July. During the last week of steam many of the footplate crews were determined to ensure steam went out in a blaze of glory, and a number of the run-down Bulleid Pacifics were pushed to exceed 100mph, a testimony to the crews' trust in their mounts.

Just four BR Standard '4MT' 4-6-0s worked through the last week of steam, and one of these, Eastleigh's double chimney-fitted No 75074, stands at Basingstoke at the head of the 06.30 Woking to Salisbury train which had started out as the 04.40 Waterloo to Woking service. No 75074 spent all its working life on the Southern Region, going new to Exmouth Junction in November 1955, and had three spells at Eastleigh and one each at Basingstoke, Stewarts Lane, Norwood Junction, and Nine Elms.

The last of the original Bulleid Light Pacifics to remain active was No 34102 *Lapford*, working out of Eastleigh shed at the time, and seen here waiting to leave Basingstoke on Monday, 3 July 1967 in charge of the 07.49 Bournemouth to Waterloo service. No 34102 is running without its nameplates and the covers over the clack valves have been removed from the top of the air-smoothed casing. Whatever their faults, the original Bulleid Pacifics were quite different to any other class of steam locomotive, and their distinctive exhaust chatter when working hard was a case of 'once heard, never forgotten'.

Ten of the BR Standard '4MT' 2-6-0s were active on the Southern Region during the last week of steam, and one of these, Bournemouth's No 76007, stands at Basingstoke after arriving with a short parcels train on Monday, 3 July 1967. Always a Southern Region-based locomotive, No 76007 went new to Eastleigh shed in January 1953, was transferred to Salisbury in May 1958, and arrived at Bournemouth in April 1967.

Southern Light Pacific No 34001 *Exeter* then appeared at the head of the 08.10 Waterloo to Weymouth train, followed by BR Standard '4MT' 2-6-0 No 76007 with a lightweight parcels train. The next down steam working arrived behind 'Merchant Navy' Pacific No 35030 *Elder Dempster Line* which was in charge of the 08.35 Waterloo to Weymouth working. With my time at Basingstoke running out I was surprised to see non-rebuilt Bulleid Light Pacific No 34102 *Lapford* drifting in with the 07.49 Bournemouth to Waterloo train. Steve had travelled back to Basingstoke behind *Lapford* to meet up with me, and we went back to Southampton behind 'Hymek' diesel-hydraulic No D7070 so that we could catch the 11.30 Weymouth to Waterloo train behind 'Merchant Navy' Pacific No 35023 *Holland Africa Line*.

In retrospect, it is a pity that we couldn't stay for a few more days, but money was tight and I had to get back to work. Stephen had been collared by a ticket inspector about ticket irregularities and was told that the Railway Police would be waiting for him at Waterloo. To avoid trouble we swapped tickets as mine had not been clipped — not a great end to our long weekend chasing Southern steam. While Stephen made his escape from Waterloo I photographed the station pilot, BR Standard '3MT' 2-6-2T No 82019. Stephen and I met up at King's Cross station for our return north behind Brush 'Type 4' diesel No D1981 to Leeds (City).

Locomotives seen on Saturday, 1 July 1967

Nine Elms shed

'West Country' Pacifics	Nos 34001, 34002, 34008, 34015, 34019, 34023, 34024, 34034, 34047, 34100.
'Battle of Britain' Pacifics	Nos 34057, 34088.
'Merchant Navy' Pacifics	Nos 35003, 35008, 35012, 35028, 35030.
Ivatt 2-6-2Ts	Nos 41284, 41312.
BR Standards	Nos 73022, 73093, 73119, 80012, 80025, 80085, 80140, 80143, 80145, 82019.
Diesels	No D3274.

Weymouth shed

'West Country' Pacifics	No 34093.
'Battle of Britain' Pacifics	No 34089.
'Merchant Navy' Pacific	No 35003, 35007, 35014, 35023, 35026.
Ivatt 2-6-2Ts	Nos 41230, 41295.
BR Standards	Nos 73002, 73016, 73093, 75056, 75068, 76006, 76008, 76069,
Diesels	Nos D2398, D6511, D6544, D7010.

Bournemouth shed

'West Country' Pacifics	Nos 34004, 34037.
Ivatt 2-6-2Ts	No 41224.
BR Standards	Nos 73020, 76005, 76009, 76026, 80011, 80134, 80146.
Diesels	Nos D2028, D2180, D2239, D2288, D6530, D6554, D7010.
Electro-diesels	Nos E6039, E6041, E6049.

Nine Elms-allocated Ivatt '2MT' class 2-6-2T No 41312 takes water at Waterloo station on Monday, 3 July 1967 while on station pilot duties. No 41312 was one of five engines of the class to make it to the end of steam, the others being Nos 41224 and 41320 at Bournemouth and Nos 41298 and 41319 at Nine Elms. No 41319 was used on the 'Kenny Belle' shuttles during the last week of steam, and was only relieved on the Friday evening workings by BR Standard '3MT' 2-6-2T No 82019.